001

Helen Fuller

Wakefield Press

Wakefield Press
16 Rose Street
Mile End
South Australia 5031
www.wakefieldpress.com.au

First published 2023

Copyright © Artist Helen Fuller, and writers Ross Wolfe, Sasha Grbich, Glenn Barkley, and Erica Green, 2023

All rights reserved. This book is copyright. Apart from any fair dealing for the purposes of private study, research, criticism or review, as permitted under the Copyright Act, no part may be reproduced without written permission. Enquiries should be addressed to the publisher.

Managing Editor — Erica Green, Director Samstag Museum of Art, University of South Australia
Editorial Assistant — Sophie Comber
Timeline text — Melinda Rackham
Image Research — Melinda Rackham and Jennifer Matthews
Consulting Editor — Lia Weston
Proofreading — Wakefield Press
Images — Courtesy the Artist and Samstag Museum of Art unless otherwise specified
Samstag Museum of Art photography — Grant Hancock
Design — Adam Johnson Design
Printing and quality control in China by Tingleman Pty Ltd

Anne & Gordon Samstag Museum of Art, 2023
University of South Australia

The Helen Fuller 2023 South Australian Living Artist Monograph has received funding from the Government of South Australia through Arts SA and University of South Australia

ISBN — 978 1 92304 201 8

A catalogue record for this book is available from the National Library of Australia

This series of books showcasing the works of South Australian living artists was initiated by the SALA Inc. Board and is published with the assistance of the Government of South Australia. This is the twenty-fourth book in the series, following; *Annette Bezor: A passionate gaze*, Richard Grayson; *Kathleen Petyarre: Genius of place*, Christine Nicholls and Ian North; *James Darling: Instinct, imagination, physical work*, Daniel Thomas; *Nick Mount: Incandescence*, Margot Osborne; *Ian W. Abdulla: Elvis has entered the building*, Stephen Fox and Janet Maughan; *Deborah Paauwe: Beautiful games*, Wendy Walker; *Michelle Nikou*, Ken Bolton; *Aldo Iacobelli: I ❤ painting*, John Neylon; *Julie Blyfield*, Stephanie Radok and Dick Richards; *Gerry Wedd: Thong cycle*, Mark Thomson; *Angela Valamanesh: About being here*, Cath Kenneally; *Khai Liew*, Peter Ward; *Hossein Valamanesh: Out of nothingness*, Mary Knights and Ian North; *Mark Kimber*, Jim Moss; *Stephen Bowers: Beyond bravura*, Damon Moon and John Neylon; *Nicholas Folland*, Lisa Slade; *Giles Bettison: Pattern and perception*, Margot Osborne; *Catherine Truman: Touching distance*, Melinda Rackham; *Christopher Orchard: The uncertainty of the poet*, Peter Goldsworthy, Margot Osborne, Roy Ananda, Julia Robinson and Rod Taylor; *Clare Belfrage: Rhythms of necessity*, Kay Lawrence and Sera Waters; *Louise Haselton: Act natural*, Gillian Brown, Leigh Robb and Jenna McKenzie; *Kirsten Coelho*, Wendy Walker; and *Mark Valenzuela*, Belinda Howden and Anna O'Loughlin.

003

Helen Fuller, 2021, hand-built terracotta, oxides, porcelain slip,
34 x 19 x 19 cm. Collection the artist. Photograph Grant Hancock.

Helen Fuller, *Five Vessels*, 2022, hand-built terracotta, oxides, porcelain slip. Powerhouse Collection. Purchased with funds from the Barry Willoughby Bequest and Powerhouse Foundation, 2022. Photograph Emma Bjorndahl.

Helen Fuller

Contents

009 **Foreword, by Erica Green**

012 Helen Fuller: Timeline 1949 —— 1978
019 Works

023 **Journey to Plenty, an essay by Ross Wolfe**

034 Helen Fuller: Timeline 1979 —— 1991
040 Works

055 **Making and Un-making Home, an essay by Sasha Grbich**

062 Helen Fuller: Timeline 1992 —— 2008
068 Works

083 **Pots, an essay by Glenn Barkley**

090 Helen Fuller: Timeline 2009 —— 2023
096 Works

128 **Samstag Museum of Art Acknowledgements**

130 **Helen Fuller Thanks**

132 **Writer Biographies**

Contents

Helen and Sootie, Tarntanya/Adelaide, South Australia, 2022.
Photograph Grant Hancock.

Helen Fuller

Foreword ¶ Although much respected in South Australia among a particular generational community, the life career of Adelaide-born Helen Fuller might have become obscured over time were it not for the opportunity of this timely SALA Monograph, which has its origin in her triumphant exhibition, *Helen Fuller*, presented by the Samstag Museum of Art for the 2022 Adelaide Festival. ¶ Fortunately, the impressive story of the artist's achievements—and, moreover, the background to her fascinating life and personal development as an artist—has now been secured for posterity. In a remarkable and adventurous life in art, stretching from her early and long association with Brisbane, commencing in 1979, and across almost the entire range of disciplines in visual art, she has remained modest to a fault, her priority always simply to be immersed in art, even if at times that placed her under the radar of public institutions. ¶ No longer. ¶ With insightful essays by writers Ross Wolfe, Sasha Grbich and Glen Barkley, the monograph illuminates Fuller's extensive career across an astonishing range of practices, from painting and assemblage, to installation-based and multimedia approaches, through to her much-celebrated late uptake of hand-formed and painted ceramics. ¶ As one essayist notes … 'Wherever she has found herself, she works—open to the forces of the day, responsive to the impulse to make and to explore … inventive and productive, unafraid to experience change.' ¶ The Samstag Museum of Art is proud to be associated with this important publication, in which Helen Fuller's vibrant personality and creative talent are present on every page. I express warm thanks to all involved.

—— *Erica Green*
Director, Anne & Gordon Samstag Museum of Art, University of South Australia

Helen Fuller, *untitled*, 2022, hand-built terracotta, porcelain slip, dimensions variable, two of three works. Queensland University of Technology Art Collection. Gift of the artist, 2023. Photograph Grant Hancock.

Helen Fuller

012

1949

Helen Fuller

1979

Timeline 1949 —— 1979

1949 ——— 1953 ¶ When Helen Fuller is born on 18 March 1949 at McBride Maternity Hospital, Medindie SA, her father instrument maker Bonython C. Fuller (Bon) is studying at university to become an engineer, while her mother Vera Knox, an award-winning midwife from Melbourne, carries out the domestic duties. Second of four (Trevor, Helen, Stan and Kip) she lives close to the beach in Glengowrie, then a rural/urban edge of Adelaide; spending time by herself, in the back-yard chook shed, up trees eating fruit and attending Methodist Sunday School. Vera sews and knits Helen's clothes while her brothers' clothing is store bought.

1954 ——— 1961 ¶ During holidays from Glenelg Primary School, Helen spends time with her paternal grandparents Maude and Percy, a cabinet-maker at Angorichina Workshop, with Percy instigating excursions to the Art Gallery of South Australia (AGSA), South Australian Museum and Maritime Museum. In summer the family takes motoring holidays to Victoria visiting her maternal grandmother Ruby. Helen delights in the annual North Terrace Flower Day displays, takes photos with her first camera, and draws on the lined and gridded cardiogram and seismograph paper her father recycles from work.

Helen Fuller

1962 ——— 1965 ¶ Enjoying art and home science at Plympton High School, cross stitching on gingham, and learning the importance of getting her knitting tension right, with Helen awarded numerous art prizes. Helen's first taste of contemporary art is illuminated photos of Mondrian paintings at David Jones Art Gallery, which she sees with Bon. A teacher's report remarks she excels at 'subjects that require the least routine effort'. Helen fails her Leaving Certificate but gains entry to South Australian School of Art (SASA), however Bon discourages art studies.

1966 ——— 1968 ¶ Taking the job closest to art and professional artists, Helen becomes a photographic re-touching artist for Adelaide Colour Laboratory, before a short stint as a clerk at the Royal Insurance Company, then becoming a Medical Illustrator for Institute of Medical Veterinary Science (IVMS) where Bon works. ¶ Her brief engagement to carpenter and champion surfer Ian 'Spud' Tait ignited a new interest and knowledge of wood and building practices, and she attended painter Lynn Collins's evening art classes at Vermont Girls Technical High School. Helen paints a large mural at Day Street Surf Club, Middleton, South Australia, in stark modernist greys, greens and black, and is renumerated with multiple bikinis and a surfboard for creating cartoons and illustrations for John Arnold's Surf Shop and *Surf-a-bout* magazine. ¶ Encouraged by Dr Earl Hackett, IMVS Deputy-Director, Helen commences part-time study at SASA, with Anatomy and Life Drawing in the 'Common' course taught by Adelaide Modernist Dora Chapman. Shy in her first life drawing class with a naked model, Helen quickly becomes excited by the discipline of drawing.

Timeline 1949 ——— 1979

1969 —— 1971 ¶ Moving towards her career as an artist, Helen studies full-time for a Teaching Diploma (Secondary Art) at Western Teachers' College, now University of South Australia (UniSA). Undertaking the art component at SASA, Helen meets ceramicist Helen McIntosh, a wonderful and supportive Design lecturer, and cherishes a pot gifted to her by McIntosh's niece. In 1970 Helen marries social worker Neil Lillecrapp, graduating in 1971 as Helen Lillecrapp-Fuller.

1974 ¶ Now a registered teacher with the South Australian Education Department, Helen teaches at Adelaide Girls High School, making her mark in school culture by painting the art room teachers' desk red! In 1974 Helen spends a term at Woodville Special School, then works briefly at Mitchell Park Technical Boys High School before resigning, knowing her passion lies elsewhere.

1975 —— 1976 ¶ While working again at IVMS, Helen travels to Europe with graphic designer John Nowland, visiting art museums in Denmark, France, Great Britain, the Netherlands and Switzerland. Inspired to continue painting, on returning to Adelaide she joins David Dallwitz, Christine Lawrence and Geoffrey Wilson on weekend painting trips in the country. Helen meets Dutch physicist/sound artist Felix Hess who later becomes her partner.

1977 ⎯⎯ 1978 ¶ Studying painting full-time at the Torrens College of Advanced Education, Adelaide (now UniSA), Helen begins making artist's books and assemblages with acrylic on board and wins the 1977 TV Channel SAS 10 Young Artists Award at the Adelaide Festival Centre Gallery, with her winning six-panel collage acquired by Flinders University. She forms an enduring friendship with fellow student Antony (Tony) Hamilton and lecturer Tony Bishop, who introduces her to art dealer Ray Hughes. She makes friends with Spanish artist Antoni Miralda at the Adelaide Festival, and becomes a member of Roundspace Studio founded by Annette Bezor and Hossein Valamanesh. Her significant affair with Tony Hamilton ends her marriage and she graduates with a Diploma of Fine Art (Painting).

1979 ¶ First solo exhibition of her collages at Ray Hughes Gallery in Brisbane, which is reviewed by art critic Gertrude Langer. University of Queensland Art Museum (UQ Art Museum) and Brisbane College of Advanced Education both acquire works from the exhibition. Travels again in Europe and the UK, and is inspired by the ceramics of Alison Britton in London. Spends three months working at Moshav Sde Nitzan, a cooperative agricultural community in Israel's Negev Desert.

Helen Fuller

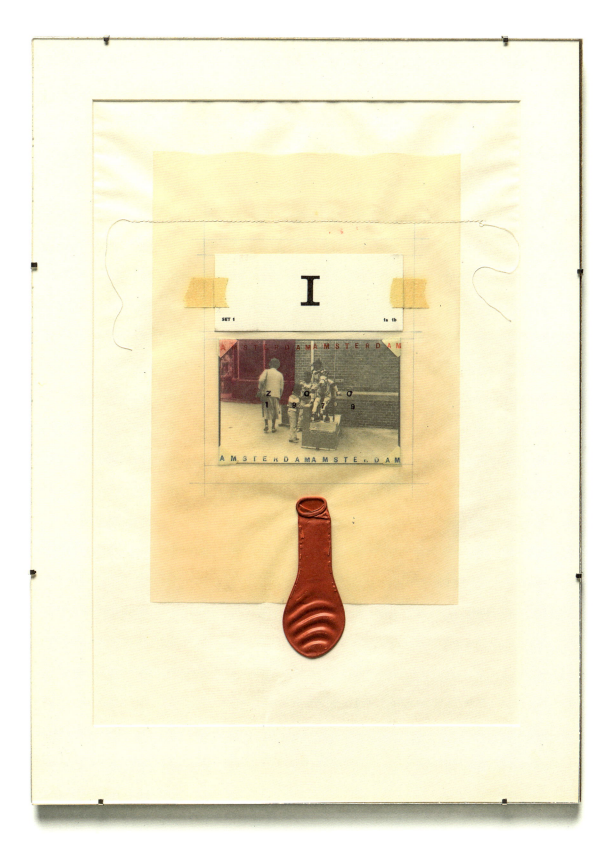

Helen Fuller, *I don't know what to do if she draws red horses and red men all the time*, 1979, collage of wax paper, photographs, printed card, balloons, adhesive tape, coloured pencil, coloured decal lettering, thread, mountboard, transparent synthetic polymer resin and metal clips, 17 panels, 40.8 x 28.8 cm (each). National Gallery of Victoria. Michell Endowment, 1980.

Helen Fuller

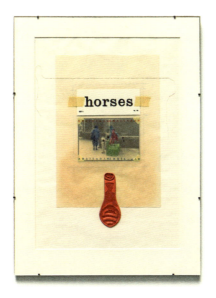

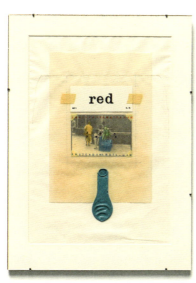

Helen Fuller, *I don't know what to do if she draws red horses and red men all the time*, 1979, collage of wax paper, photographs, printed card, balloons, adhesive tape, coloured pencil, coloured decal lettering, thread, mountboard, transparent synthetic polymer resin and metal clips, 17 panels, 40.8 × 28.8 cm (each). National Gallery of Victoria. Michell Endowment, 1980.

Helen Fuller

> "We all make our choices, and those choices put us on a road."
>
> Mike Ehrmantraut
> *Better Call Saul*, season 5

Helen Fuller: Journey to Plenty
essay by Ross Wolfe

Helen Fuller welcomes me to her Goodwood, Adelaide, home with an apology: 'I hope you'll excuse the mess. I haven't had time to clean!'[1] Sootie, the artist's constant companion, has already announced my arrival, barking furiously well before I've even lifted the gate latch, but now she sniffs my legs in cautious recognition.

We pause in the small front yard to consider the giant persimmon and quince trees planted by Fuller years ago, and which bear so much seasonal fruit that it's a challenge for her to give it away. It's a sign of the fecundity to come.

When Fuller says 'mess', I know what she means. A first-time visitor entering the house would likely be awed by the artist's habitat, each room boasting wall-to-wall displays of fascinating miscellany—comprised largely of found things picked up on habitual visits to second-hand stores, co-mingled with *objets d'art*; works of art by friends, associates and herself. It's a vast, eclectic collection that speaks of sensibility, decorative fervour and a compulsive addiction to curios that resonate with aesthetic value and personal meaning.

She'd call herself a hoarder, however it's a misnomer. The Fuller home may be visually intense, but, like so much of her art, it is coherent and orderly. Procured with evident discernment, individual objects lure the visitor to stop, and to inspect, their placement a room-by-room curatorial exercise!

It's my first visit to the Fuller residence in some years—too long, I realise—yet much is familiar, and it rekindles memories. Once, at Festival time in 2004, we shared a marvellous summer dinner here on the back porch with Fuller friends Bill and Shirley Robinson, visiting from Queensland for Bill's exhibition, *The Revelation of Landscape,* at the University of South Australia Art Museum, all of us trading yarns over wine with Dave Hickey, the great American cultural critic brought to Adelaide by Erica Green for that year's Artists' Week.

He must surely have wondered where he was.[2]

Fuller knew Robinson from her time teaching painting with him, on and off for several years until 1991, at the Queensland University of Technology (QUT) school of art in Brisbane.[3] They remain close.[4]

Her long relationship with Brisbane began in 1979, soon after Ray Hughes—the late legendary gallerist renowned for his 'good eye', who was in Adelaide looking for fresh talent—was brought by influential local sculptor Tony Bishop through the South Australian School of Art (SASA) studios at Stanley Street, where Fuller was just completing her fine art studies. Hughes invited her to exhibit at his eponymous Brisbane gallery, and continued to do so in subsequent years. It was respect.

Hughes also took Fuller's work to Sydney—along with that of Brisbane artists such as Robinson, Davida Allen, Robert McPherson, Madonna Staunton and Joe Furlonger—after famously purchasing Rudy Komon's venerated old Paddington establishment in 1985, three years after Komon's death. The bold intrusion on hallowed Sydney turf by an invading provincial was reminiscent of Kym Bonython's shock takeover of the Hungry Horse Gallery twenty years before, and was noticed. It leveraged both Hughes himself and his stable of out-of-town artists, previously unseen in Sydney.

'Ray was fun to be with,' Fuller says, 'at least early in the relationship. He had enthusiasm and loved to chat, in fact, he was great! I moved to Brisbane in 1980 after that first show, and I rented a small house near to Ray's gallery in Red Hill. He gave me a kitten as a house-warming gift, a beautiful pedigree Burmese that I named Grey Cat. The Ray Hughes Gallery was a hub of social activity where you'd meet people. He'd bring influential artworld curators who were visiting Brisbane to the house—people such as Elwyn Lynn and Nick Waterlow—to show them my new work. He even sent his partner and future wife, Annette, for me to show her how to sew and to make scrambled eggs.'

It was her collage works that had caught Ray Hughes's attention. Pasting and plastering things down on paper—playing with materials. She enjoyed the tactility of mulching stuff up, too, and layering the result experimentally on surfaces to see how it looked. However, by the time the Art Gallery of New South Wales's internationally respected curator Bernice Murphy invited Fuller into her distinguished second biennial survey, *Australian Perspecta 1983*—sharing the stage with luminaries such as Marina Abramović and Ulay, Colin Lanceley, Gareth Sansom, Robert Hunter and Robert Klippel (and soon-to-bes, including Dale Frank, Susan Norrie, Hossein Valamanesh, and Julie Rrap[5])—it had become assemblages.

Found things, attached to other found things; twigs and sticks, skewered with horsehair, gripped by rubber, painted and wired—a conversation of materials organised elegantly into crafted timber boxes lined with intriguing but inscrutable parchments from an old Arabic medical book, discovered by Fuller in an abandoned house. Echoes of Joseph Cornell and Kurt Schwitters, with just the hint, perhaps, of a Christo maquette.

She had a feel for it—an eye for the abstract material oddity—and scrupulous presentation. Thoughtful. Probing. Looking for a way forward. Early days!

Over lunch at Goodwood, we chat more about her personal history, extensive travels and career.

I learn that it was her paternal grandfather, a cabinet-maker, who first nurtured her interest in art, taking her on visits to the Art Gallery of South Australia and the South Australian Museum. That on finishing high school in 1965, where she'd won numerous prizes for art and gained entry (so young) into the South Australian School of Art (SASA), she was thwarted by parental opposition and instead found employment in art-related roles, such as in photographic laboratories and as an illustrator at the Institute of Medical and Veterinary Science.[6]

It was nonetheless valuable experience. Determined, she began studying part-time at SASA, eventually gaining an art-teaching qualification through the Western Teachers' College.[7] She had a work ethic.

In 1970, at the age of twenty-one and now free to leave the parental home, she married Neil Lillecrapp, a social worker,[8] and for a while taught art in secondary schools around Adelaide. It gave her independence, but by 1976 she'd had enough and headed off on her first overseas adventure, visiting art museums in Europe and Great Britain.

Inspired, she returned to Adelaide and full-time study at SASA under Tony Bishop, forming a close personal bond with fellow student Antony Hamilton. And then, in 1979, Ray Hughes arrived, the relationship opening her up to a wider world of professional art and artists.

Not everyone got along with the notoriously rambunctious Queensland art dealer, who—despite his generous sociability as a host and the genuine loyalty he commanded from his artists—could be unpleasantly rude and alienating. But Fuller managed it.[9] Significantly, works from that first exhibition in Brisbane were acquired for public collections. Over the coming years, more would follow.

Newly confident and hungry for experience, Fuller returned to Europe and England later that year, even spending three months in an Israeli *moshav*— a cooperative agricultural community.

In Berlin, she had the good fortune to meet René Block, the distinguished German curator and gallerist, who, by chance, was that evening opening a Joseph Beuys exhibition, *Ja, jetzt brechen wir hier den Scheiß ab*,[10] at his Galerie René Block. He invited her in for a preview at the closed gallery. It was the best kind of education.

It had been Block, in fact, who'd famously introduced Beuys to America in 1974 with his legendary performance work *I Like America and America Likes Me*, in which Beuys spent eight hours a day, over three days, confined with a coyote in Block's Manhattan SoHo gallery.[11]

Helen Fuller outside the Adelaide Railway Station going to the South Australian School of Art, 1971.

The European artists interested Fuller more than most. She'd met Nikolaus Lang and Romanian-born Swiss artist Daniel Spoerri in 1978 at Tony Bishop's house in Adelaide during her art studies at SASA, the two men travelling the country in association with Nick Waterlow's forthcoming *3rd Biennale of Sydney: European Dialogue*.

Lang, a German artist, had long been interested in visiting Parachilna in South Australia's Flinders Ranges to find 'the holy colour' of earth associated with Aboriginal people local to that area that he'd once read about.[12]

Helen Fuller: Journey to Plenty

Spoerri's domestic-focussed work would especially have impacted on Fuller. On the Biennale's opening night, he hosted a lavish dinner for art cognoscenti inside the Art Gallery of New South Wales (AGNSW), and later glued the remains—the china, cutlery, and glass, etc., the mess of it all—onto several tablecloths and had these fastened to the gallery wall.[13] It was a different kind of art.

Beuys, too, participated in Waterlow's *European Dialogue* with an 'action' work, *Ausfegen*[14], of street rubbish swept with a red-bristled broom into a pile alongside the gallery wall, accompanied by the broom. Rich in installation art as it was, the 1979 Biennale of Sydney was a revelation for Australian artists.

Soon enough, inevitably, Australia drew Fuller back from her travels in Europe. In 1980, she divorced her husband of ten years, ripping up and burning her wedding dress.[15]

She embarked on a roaming, itinerate lifestyle, travelling frequently between Melbourne, Brisbane and Adelaide. Excursions with Antony Hamilton to Moonta—an old mining town on South Australia's Yorke Peninsula coast—were important, not only providing her with materials and ideas for work but also nurturing a relationship of enduring depth with Hamilton.

Travel and 'hanging about' have been hallmarks of Fuller's adult life. She suggests it was her childhood—overbearing parental authority spawned gnawing discontent and habitual restlessness.

Her father, she says, not only dismissed her interest in art but also appropriated the paintings she'd made on hardboard in high school, repurposing them as bland cupboard doors for his shed. Her mother, too, imposed a regime of stultifying ordinariness on her creative daughter, dressing her in homemade clothes that Fuller despised, regarding them as 'hideous'!

That may explain the hidden dark side to her, unknown to most—a wilful instinct to pit the self against the forces of life regardless of consequence, perhaps as a way, obliquely, to learning and knowledge. And where some see a retiring personality clothed in privacy, friends see the humorous candour and the dangerous, biting wit.

A shrewd and critical observer, the artist knows she has seen a bigger world.

Fuller had been to Melbourne often—the city was one of her favourite places in which to 'hang about and think', as she very much liked to do. Time to park the wanderlust for a while, aided by house-sitting. She had also developed several friendships there with fellow artists; it came easily.

When she needed money, she'd look for jobs of a kind that required low commitment. At one stage in Melbourne, typically supporting herself, she'd even worked as a builder's labourer, channelling the spirit of that strange *sadhu* Ian Fairweather and his hard labour on Darwin's hot council roads, as he secretly prepared for his astonishing raft journey, out past the harbour crocodiles in moonlight and to the dark ocean beyond.

Late 1983 found Fuller in North Queensland and the Northern Territory, travelling with Felix Hess, a Dutch Fluxus artist and physicist she'd first met in Adelaide back in 1976. He was interested in Zen philosophy and collected Aboriginal art. Together, they made sound recordings of frogs.

Helen Fuller, *Sticks and Stones*, 1982, boxed assemblage: stick, horsehair, wire, balloon fragments, newspaper, castration ring, sheet of Arabic text, stones, nine panels, each panel, 32.8 x 23.0 x 6.5 cm. Private Collection, Brisbane.

The following year, she was away again with Hess, first to Groningen in the Netherlands and then to Berlin, where he was selling his frog recordings at Ursula Block's experimental music store, gelbe MUSIK. Berlin was alive with avant-garde culture. Invited to a Merce Cunningham Dance Company rehearsal at Freie Volksbühne (the Free People's Theatre), they had tea and conversation with John Cage, who was interested in Hess's work and potentially in collaborating with him.

For Helen Fuller, the artist, it had become an adventurous, searching life. Whatever it was that fundamentally motivated her, it seemed that, above all, the choices she made were for the pursuit of new experience and, instinctively, change. Like a secular travelling monk, she eschewed security and the conventions of career, other than for her abiding desire to make art. Of course, given her lifestyle and material constraints, that most often meant working from a travelling bag, Schwitters-like, in small rooms.

Returning to Australia, she unexpectedly found work as a graphic artist for the National Trust at Gulf Station, a farm in Yarra Glen on the outskirts of Melbourne. She was thirty-five. It was a flexible arrangement that enabled her to come and go.

Sure enough, by 1985 she was back in Brisbane, living in a shared Kangaroo Point warehouse with artist friends Stephen Killick, Tom Risley and Jo Davidson, collecting stuff from second-hand stores to resource her practice and teaching art part-time at Brisbane College of Advanced Education.

By now she had much of value to offer her students.

Later that year, on a visit to Adelaide for Christmas with friends, she ran into Dick Richards, the curator of Asian art at the Art Gallery of South Australia and a person of influence in the development of Adelaide's original JamFactory.

They had mutual friends, notably Richards's ex-wife Edit, who was then living in Brisbane and married to artist Lawrence Daws. Richards alerted Fuller to a significant archaeological project in Thailand with which he and Don Hein, a fellow AGSA professional, were involved.

Helen Fuller, *Small Dutch composite no. 1*, 1984, oil on thick woven paper, one of twelve panels, each 18 x 13 cm. Queensland University of Technology Art Collection. Gift of the artist, 1990. Photograph Louis Lim.

The project, sponsored by Adelaide cultural institutions, involved the recovery of buried ceramics and artefacts at a village called Ban Ko Noi, 500 kilometres north-east of Bangkok on a tributary of the Mekong River. Ancient kilns and beautifully decorated thirteenth-century ceramics had been found at the site, which was not previously known as a pottery production centre for the rich trade in South East Asian ceramics of that era. It had been an historic discovery.

Asia hadn't been on her radar. It was an educational diversion.

A final adventure with Antony Hamilton—travelling to Cooper Creek and Lake Killalpaninna in South Australia's arid north—confirmed the limits of the relationship. Hamilton, a born mystic, had a deep and abiding longing for immersion in the Australian landscape; it was not uncommon for him simply to up and disappear.

'He was very good to be with in the bush,' Fuller says. 'He had an innate sense of where he was, and an inner connection to place, and he was good at finding things, particularly Aboriginal peoples' relics, although I only later understood that these should be left where they were. We'd camp with a swag. He would do the cooking. Tony was a hard man in his way, and we would do it rough. He would never tell anyone where he was going!'[16]

But no matter what his fealty to Fuller, she saw he would forever first be drawn to his own, uncompromising vision. She'd known it all along: there was no real future in it.

By 1989, Fuller was lecturing full-time in art at the Brisbane College of Advanced Education—soon to merge with the QUT—where she was able to closely observe an intriguing colleague, Gwyn Hanssen Pigott, at her ceramics craft. Pigott warranted respect; she'd once worked as a maker at Bernard Leach's pottery in Cornwall.

'She was so scatty in life,' Fuller recalls of Pigott, 'but to watch her at work—calm, centred and controlled, elevating ceramics as art—was impressive.' It was a spirit she admired, and an influence she acknowledges.

Early in 1990, Fuller met David Zhu, a Chinese graphic artist and calligrapher recently arrived from Shanghai to study the English language. They had a mutual friend in Joe Deville, the Queensland Art Gallery exhibitions designer, who'd met Zhu in Shanghai and encouraged his interest in coming to Brisbane.[17] After Tiananmen Square and the memory of his father's suffering as a victim of the Cultural Revolution, Zhu needed little convincing.

There was frisson. Fuller and Zhu married in October that year in Brisbane. By Christmas, she was pregnant, and, in September 1991, had a child, Alexander.

———

For all her comings and goings, Fuller had consolidated her reputation in Brisbane as a local artist of importance. With the continuing backing of Ray Hughes Gallery, local curators increasingly sought her out to participate in mixed shows at public galleries, not least at the Queensland Gallery of Art.

Fuller's art practice, up until then, had been shaped by her unsettled lifestyle. It followed a template she'd laid down early: the work was generally modest in scale, and its content of blended elements largely drew on domestic themes, imaginatively animated by diverse media such as collage and painting, or assemblages made from op-shop bric-a-brac and found things.

Invariably, the foundation impulse in her work was one of patterning and orderly structure. According to Fuller, it was a predisposition that she'd inherited from her father, Bonython C. Fuller (BCF).

The QUT, where Fuller now worked, already hosted an important collection of Australian art—including several of her works—and an ambitious university art museum was being planned. Fuller's colleague and friend Stephen Rainbird, a curator of art at the university, persuaded QUT to sponsor a major survey of her work. The exhibition, *Helen Lillecrapp-Fuller: A Visual Diary 1979-91*, would premiere at the Queensland Art Gallery (in lieu of the still-under-construction QUT Art Museum) in August 1991, and thereafter travel to regional centres in Queensland.[18]

The first such exhibition to be undertaken by QUT, *A Visual Diary*, was a triumph for Fuller; it distinguished her.

Rainbird not only effectively illuminated the artist's oeuvre to 1991 but had also thoroughly researched Fuller's history and concerns, documenting these in an informative catalogue.

The exhibition's timing was serendipitous, occurring just as Fuller had become a mother. However, it was also to be the end of a cycle. Regardless of artistic achievement and real-world experience, art school academics were now required to boast post-graduate Masters degrees.

Her contract at the newly merged QUT was not being renewed.

And so she returned to Adelaide. There was, after all, nowhere else to go. *A Visual Diary* would be Fuller's farewell to Brisbane.

———

Helen Fuller, *BCF*, 1995, installation view, UniSA Art Museum, mixed media. Photograph Michal Kluvanek.

Not one to sit idle, in 1992 Fuller enrolled in SASA's freshly minted Master of Visual Art degree at the newly formed University of South Australia (UniSA), with which SASA had been merged the year before.

Midway through the two-year program, she learned that an application made for an Asialink-sponsored artist-in-residency project at the Zhejiang Academy of Fine Arts in Hangzhou, China, had been successful. The director of Asialink, Alison Carroll—a former senior curator at the Art Gallery of South Australia—had approached Fuller early in 1992, encouraging her to apply.

Fuller's Mandarin-speaking husband, David, would enhance the opportunity; it would be a team effort, too good to resist. And so, the Masters was temporarily deferred and the family headed off to a four-month sojourn in Hangzhou.

The Zhejiang Academy proved ill-prepared to host such a project, and Fuller was left to make her own arrangements. 'Everything was unsophisticated,' she recalls, the facilities 'broken and primitive', with only cold water for amenity. With few options, she walked the streets, filling a sketchbook and observing the life around her—'the ducks, the people and the washing'.

Through David's crucial mediating role they made do, gradually finding resources, including an abundant supply of hand-made rice paper which enabled some paintings and collages. They would bring a huge stock of the paper back with them to Adelaide; it would anchor an important strand in her future practice.

By the completion of the SASA Masters program, Fuller had reinvented herself radically. The mature artist was emerging.

The change began with her inspired adoption of fabrics—dresses, rags and gingham tablecloths—as both subject and medium. Her pregnancy—and, later, her post-natal body—gave her a new introspection, a new way of looking at domesticity and her changed life as a mother. Clothes that once fitted no longer did.

There was additionally the lovely damask linen she'd inherited from kindly Nanna Maude, her late paternal grandmother with whom she'd stayed on school holidays from the age of five, which had poignant significance. Nanna also had a button box, and Fuller, the child, would play happily with the buttons for hours, making floral patterns.[19]

Fabrics and rags became vocabulary. She would cut them up and reassemble them—paint and sew on them, attach things to them. Fabric was an enabling revelation to Fuller; it provided a fecund link to her inner life, fuelling a range of works and ideas that she would carry well into the future.

In a sad coincidence, Fuller's father had died the same day in 1991 that Alexander was born, opening the artist to reflections on his parental influence. She had experienced grief. Long after returning to Adelaide it lay heavy on her.

Significantly, her father—BCF—had been unsupportive of his daughter's aspiration for a life in art. And although Fuller had nevertheless done what she wished despite him, the father's influence—and his unusual, dominating personality—had in many ways still determined her course.

Helen Fuller: BCF, her major solo exhibition presented at the University of South Australia Art Museum in 1995, was as much a Freudian cleansing as an affectionate visual memoir of her father.[20] It also signalled Fuller's shift to installation, a medium—like the fabric—that would preoccupy and reward her over the coming decade.

An engineer and medical instrument-maker, BCF had carried his professional interests into retirement, filling his home-based shed with all the machinery and apparatus that might be needed for ambitious making. He was obsessional. Comprehensive records of his sometimes-peculiar interests were also kept in immaculately labelled hanging files, sorted alphabetically: *Bridge Failures; Expatriation; Gilbert & Sullivan Society; Home Improvements Ideas; Incinerators; Investment Ideas; Mementos of Memory; Men of Destiny; Mineralogy; Physiological Parameters; Speech-Making Rules*, to name a few.

BCF saved things—in fact, pretty much everything. 'He never threw anything away,' Fuller recalled, 'including toothbrushes and brooms.'

But his shed was tidy and orderly. Helen, the daughter, the child, snuck in when he wasn't there. 'It was a playground,' she says. 'A wonderland!'

In an ambitious plan, Fuller transported almost the entirety of the BCF shed to the UniSA Art Museum gallery (then in suburban Underdale) and distributed its contents widely around the cavernous exhibition space.[21] She then set to work, contriving her own whimsical narrative from her father's treasured things.

Ross Wolfe

She made a sham shed.

It was a BCF takeover. Bins and cupboard drawers lay everywhere, some arrayed on timber planks supported by tins of White Wings soup mix. Machines that linked to lights which served no apparent purpose. Vintage radio magazines displayed in plastic sheaths covered acres of gridded wall space. Pantihose stretched ridiculously across the gallery floor, reaching for the wall.

Fuller had undone her father's empire of fastidious order with a faux-industrial parody. If there was a rationale, it was absurdist, a Dadaist poem. For the artist, a turning point. Over the next several years, the BCF project would provide a recurring, fertile touchstone for Fuller.

Helen Fuller, Penance, 2004, installation view, UniSA Art Museum, white cotton industrial rags, timber slats and mirror, plastic buckets. Photograph Helen Fuller.

Bless This Mess, her contribution to Juliana Engberg's *All this and Heaven too: 1998 Adelaide Biennial of Australian Art* at the Art Gallery of South Australia, was effectively a reconfigured BCF shed, writ small. The installation comprised a mock backyard barbeque made of books sourced from BCF's vast collection, accompanied by two interfacing, four-drawer filing cabinets, filled with his systematically labelled hanging files.

Another exhibition at AGSA two years later, *Chemistry: Art in South Australia 1990–2000*, surveyed the work of over seventy artists who'd comprised the backbone of contemporary practice in the state during the decade to 2000. It was an important show; many of the works—including one by Fuller—had been acquired through the generous Faulding 150 Anniversary Fund.

Fuller's work in *Chemistry*, *... a cow of a thing*, purchased by AGSA in 1995, had in fact originally been a component of the BCF exhibition. It was a strange thing indeed: a transmogrified table, cluttered with personal signifiers.

Fuller had dangled a camera beneath the table, along with pieces of miniature furniture taken from a child's doll's house. Two legs of the table were wrapped protectively in fabric: there were also boxes, a light and a chair. Everything was underneath. A suite of BCF's hanging files stretched between table and wall, suspended like a piano accordion.

The idea of the table still had currency for Fuller almost a decade later. Her complex 2004 installation, *Penance*—in a group exhibition[22] at the by-then city-based UniSA Art Museum—featured white cotton industrial rags pulled forcefully through a slatted timber table.

The rag tops protruding above the table formed into small, triangular, shell-like shapes, set neatly in a grid pattern that became the shape of a cross. Underneath the table the rags remained unfurled, making a dense mass like subterranean stalactites. The four table legs each sat on upturned, menstrual-red buckets, and a large gilt-framed mirror placed beneath the table on the floor reflected upwards, voyeuristically.

More rags ran along an adjoining wall, like washing on a line, while nearby to the table a red laundry trolley (sans basket) was swamped by a mound of yet more rags—these, however, individually rolled and neatly bound by a red thread.

Finally, on another wall, a selection of framed paintings on Chinese paper featured abstract, cross-hatched patterns, some embellished with buttons and safety pins.

A clearly gendered statement, rich in domestic signifiers, the *Penance* installation was at once inviting of engagement, yet inscrutable. It was also emblematic of the concerns that, by and large, had sustained Fuller's artistic journey for several years following her return to Adelaide in 1991.

Two decades on, Fuller's marriage was under pressure: there were corrosive disagreements and divergent interests. It took a toll. She turned inwards—eschewing the art world, limiting her social life to siblings and just a few steadfast friends.

In 2010, she found a diversion that got her away from town, at least for a while, providing fieldwork photography for her researcher friend Dr Keryn Walshe at the Nullarbor Plain's remote Koonalda Cave. Located on Mirning country and sixty metres below ground—mostly in darkness—the cave was mined for flint by Aboriginal people 30,000 years ago. They traded the valuable material to communities far afield.[23]

But, rewarding as it was, Fuller needed something more permanent, something different to help shake off the black dog that had periodically wrapped itself around her from a young age.

She wandered into a pottery hobby class in the Adelaide suburbs.

———

We've finished lunch and agree that it's time to look at pots.

Since the 2009 hobby class at Burnside's Hubbe Court, Fuller has been experimenting with forms, patterning and surface treatments, but also with the ceramic craft itself, endeavouring to master it. Her knowledge and technique have evolved. She's come to like clay's responsiveness and plasticity and its 'intriguing possibilities', and is by now fully immersed. It is her dominant interest.

There have been several exhibitions, not least at the Australian National University's renowned Drill Hall Gallery in Canberra, in 2014.[24]

More recently, the preparations for an exhibition at the University of South Australia's prestigious Samstag Museum of Art have absorbed her. Presented during the 2022 Adelaide Festival, in an innovative display conceived by her colleague, designer Khai Liew, it proved a celebrated coming-out.

We head to the studio—it's at the back of the yard through a calming jungle of trees and plants. There'd once been a bit of lawn here, I recall. No more. A huge melaleuca paperbark arches above, thriving in the lush Adelaide backyard; it must be fifty years old. A wattlebird squawks an alert as we pass below.

We enter the studio and, gazing about, I realise that I am in Helen Fuller's land of plenty. Hand-built terracotta ceramics, years of completed work, are neatly arrayed on shelves; wrapped, waiting.

It's a breathtaking surprise: all her accumulated past of making and her vast experience, skills, and knowledge have coalesced into this.

She brings them out; one by one they are patiently unwrapped.

There is something magical about Helen Fuller's unusual ceramics, and something compelling as well in the way they manifest such strange forms and visual effects. It's as if the artist has drawn upon a store of secret knowledge from the liminal zone—or paid the devil—releasing a power by which the work is imbued with mysterious meaning.

The 'pots', as she calls them, are all over the shop, defying easy categorisation. Their impulse is essentially sculptural more so than decorative, although colour plays a role. Random, surprising things, they are individuals from an uncommon tribe, their personalities both light and dark. This elegant blue one here, for example—a study in pure, simple happiness—clearly has the sun in it. And the one there, with the dark spirit, surely suggests archaeological and ancestral matter—ghosts, past lives of kin, or urns for the beloved dead.

Then again, look more deeply, and perhaps it cries for the unknowability of ancient Indigenous minds.

Whatever it is that inspires them, Fuller's pots are very beautiful, albeit in an unconventional way. That is their gift.

Helen Fuller, *Hand-built vessel*, 2021, hand-built terracotta with underglaze, oxides, porcelain slip, 21.6 x 21.7 x 22.7 cm. Art Gallery of South Australia Collection. Edward Minton Newman Bequest Fund 2022. Photograph Grant Hancock.

The poet Les Murray once described his preparation for creative work as sitting quietly at table with his materials—the pencil and paper—ready. He said the verse came largely unbidden from the back of his head, rather than the conscious, reasoning mind—a creation almost of its own that he knowingly facilitated. His poetry, he said, was produced in 'a trance'.[25] All that he contributed or needed, he implied, was intent.

Fuller's pots begin similarly, in the most elementary manner. She lays down a looping coil of soft terracotta clay on her studio banding wheel, and then another, and more, and so on, gradually working it all up. It's a meditation.

There might be a thought as a starting point, to provide intention—most often the patterns and textures of organic things, such as seed pods and plants that she's found when out doggie-walking Sootie.

As her hands touch the clay, though, it could as likely be her late father's ever-remembered shed, or her grandmother Nanna Maude speaking to her of damask and gingham fabrics.

Always, there is memory.

Ross Wolfe

After a while, something is formed, comes to life on the wheel. She might then draw into the object, scribing or physically impressing a pattern—shaping. Later, after the bisque firing, she will consider her options. Typically—though not exclusively—her choice is a commercial oxide underglaze applied by brush. She'll work the surface some more. A favourite treatment is the bleed-through, a ghostly semi-transparent stain that reveals an alluring hint of the terracotta base, achieved with a slip she's made using porcelain tailings from the studio of her friend Kirsten Coelho.

When something goes wrong or she becomes bored—and if the pot is still damp—it can lead to play and experiment—'fiddling around,' she calls it. Something new then starts to happen, and another journey begins.

Most recently, Fuller's been travelling, on and off, to Beltana, a largely deserted town in South Australia's arid mid-north, ancestral home to the Adnyamathanha people, fulfilling her commitment as executor for the estate of her friend Antony Hamilton following his untimely death in 2020.

It enriches her.

An austere place, to the casual eye there's not much to see in Beltana, other than for Hamilton's windowless stone railway worker's cottage. Along with his previously unseen artworks, it's all been entrusted to Fuller's safe hands to make sense of.

On her last visit, she cast his ashes to the wind, as he wanted, and watched them disappear into the afternoon haze of the Flinders Ranges landscape.

Helen Fuller's life journey in art is now well past forty years. Wherever she has found herself, she works—open to the forces of the day, responsive to the impulse to make and to explore. She is inventive and productive, unafraid to experience change, even though—like a monk—she fervently eschews the public arena.

Make no mistake, though—most days she will be found in her studio, immersed in the deep well of her life of plenty, the force of her imaginative practice as steady as sunshine.

—— ***Ross Wolfe***

Ross Wolfe

1. Unless otherwise noted, all quotes are by Helen Fuller, from conversations with the author, variously, 2021 and 2022.

2. Described by critic Peter Schjeldahl as 'the philosopher king of American art criticism', Dave Hickey (d 2021) was the principal speaker at the 2004 Artists' Week, curated by Erica Green, then director of the University of South Australian Art Museum (now the Samstag Museum of Art).

3. Fuller had met Robinson and his wife Shirley at the Ray Hughes Gallery, and she remembers they quickly became friends. It had been Bill Robinson and his close colleague Merve Muhling—a former art teacher of Ray Hughes's—who together enabled Fuller's original teaching opportunity at the then Brisbane College of Advanced Education, which merged in 1990 with the Queensland University of Technology.

4. After Shirley Robinson's death in March 2022, the QUT Art Museum produced a special exhibition in her honour, *Love in Life & Art* (October 2022), featuring works by Bill Robinson that celebrated their shared family life. The exhibition was accompanied by a substantial illustrated publication with memorial essays by a small number of close Robinson friends, including Dame Quentin Bryce AD CVO. At Bill Robinson's request, Fuller, too, contributed a memoir—*Reflection*.

5. Born Julie Parr, she in fact exhibited in *Perspecta 83* as Julie Brown, reflecting her marriage at the time to artist Bill Brown, later changing her name to Julie Rrap.

6. Her duties included making sketches in pencil and watercolour showing the anatomical structure of the human body to aid lectures and research.

7. At the time, SASA was administered by the state Education Department and its pre-eminent role was to support art teacher training. It was only following institutional amalgamations that SASA secured sufficient independence to conduct a comprehensive fine art program designed for the professional training of artists.

8. They were married at St Peter's College Chapel in Adelaide. A graduate of the prestigious school, Lillecrapp was widely regarded for his high-achieving leadership in sports.

9. Her final exhibition with Hughes was in Sydney in 1987, after which her forbearance was exhausted. Fuller recalls: 'Eventually his other side emerged; he was easily threatened, for example, if you became friendly with someone with whom he'd fallen out. And he'd keep insisting that you accompany him to strip clubs at the drop of a hat, but once was more than enough for me! It all ended after that final show at his Sydney gallery in 1987—the old Rudy Komon Gallery—when we went to the Taxi Club. There was just too much booze and bad boy behaviour, and I wrote him a letter terminating the relationship. When Ray was good, he was great, but if he turned on you, he was cruel. He didn't seem to have any social filters; it was as if he was constantly testing your limits of tolerance. But nevertheless, I have to say, Ray was great, at least for a time!'

10. That is: 'Yeah, now we're breaking shit here!'

11. Later, as director of Berlin's daadgalerie, Block featured several Australian artists in projects such as *Fünf vom Fünften* (*Five from the Fifth*), 1985. He was also the first foreign artistic director of a Biennale of Sydney—*Art is Easy: The Readymade Boomerang*, in 1990.

12. Lang's Biennale installation work—*Samples of Earth, Colours and Paintings*—combined European earth pigments collected near Tuscany with 'earth colours' that he collected south of Adelaide. Lang later wrote that he'd long been attracted to visiting Australia after reading in 1968 about migrating Australian Aboriginal people, and 'a place, Parachilna, in Southern Australia, to which a holy colour of the natives was ascribed'. See Nikolaus Lang in 'Visitors: Reactions/Letters', a post-Biennale compendium of reviews, *European Dialogue: A Commentary, 3rd Biennale of Sydney*, November 1979, p.57.

13. Spoerri also gained from his time in South Australia, finding the much-dehydrated corpse of a cow on a visit to the Flinders, which he transported to the AGNSW and displayed on a carpet before a live television set.

14. That is: 'The Sweeping Out'.

15. Fuller recalls her friend Lawrence Daws saying at the time, 'fire is cleansing!' She later incorporated parts of the torn and burnt dress into assemblages, some of which are now in the QUT Art Museum collection.

16. For an account of the artist's career, see Wolfe, R., 'Tribute: Antony Hamilton 1955–2020', *Art Monthly Australasia*, Winter 2021, p.94.

17. Deville had been in Shanghai to help prepare and condition-report the exhibition *Treasures from the Shanghai Museum* that was to travel to the Queensland Art Gallery. Zhu's brother Christopher (his Anglicised *nom de guerre*) was deputy director at the Shanghai Museum, and a respected past visiting scholar at Princeton University.

18. Although she had divorced Neil Lillecrapp in 1980, Fuller's gallerist, Ray Hughes, had for years insisted she retain the hyphenated 'Lillecrapp-Fuller' designation, for the reason that she'd established her artistic identity in this manner. *A Visual Diary* would be the last occasion that Fuller presented herself this way.

19. Helen Fuller, from a Wilderness School Art Forum program, May 2003.

20. For an insightful interpretation of the exhibition, see Fazakerley, R., 'Helen Fuller', in *Helen Fuller: BCF*, (exhibition catalogue), University of South Australian Art Museum, 1995.

21. In 1995 the UniSA Art Museum was located at UniSA's Underdale campus, alongside the SASA, but relocated in 1998 to a temporary, converted warehouse on North Terrace, popularly known for its former business name, *Tiles of Distinction*. In 2007 the Anne & Gordon Samstag Museum of Art was established in new, purpose-built premises on the same UniSA City West campus site.

22 Fuller was one of three artists in the exhibition *From the Ephemeral to the Eternal: The recent work of Eugene Carchesio, Helen Fuller and Madonna Staunton* at the UniSA Art Museum, 2004, curated by Stephen Rainbird.

23 See Walshe, K., 'Koonalda Cave, Nullarbor Plain, South Australia – Issues in Optical and Radiometric Dating of Deep Karst Caves', *Geochronometria*, vol. 44, 2017, pps.366-373.

24 The important Drill Hall Gallery opportunity followed Fuller's introduction to Drill Hall director, Terence Maloon, by their mutual friend Ingrid Kellenbach, then CEO of Adelaide Central School of Art. Exhibitions by Fuller at the Adelaide Central Gallery, prior to this, were among the earliest occasions that she publicly presented her ceramic works.

25 From an interview with Les Murray for the BBC Desert Island Disks program, BBC Radio 4, 21 August, 1998 <https://www.bbc.co.uk/programmes/p00942zs>

1980

Helen Fuller

1991

Timeline 1980 —— 1991

1980 ¶ Divorces Neil Lillecrapp and burns her wedding dress, saving the ash for use in future artworks. Moves to Brisbane with offer of part-time teaching (painting/drawing/sculpture) at Brisbane College of Advanced Education, now Queensland University of Technology (QUT), working with colleagues Gwyn Hanssen Pigott, Merv Muhling and William (Bill) Robinson, who later becomes a close friend. Her artwork in the major survey *Drawn and Quartered: Australian Contemporary Paperwork* at Art Gallery of South Australia (AGSA) is acquired by National Gallery of Victoria (NGV).

1981 ——— 1982 ¶ During excursions to Yorke Peninsula with Tony Hamilton, gathers objects at Moonta Rubbish Tip for her assemblages. Group shows in Adelaide, Brisbane and Sydney. Meets artists Yvonne Boag and Robert Hunter while visiting Melbourne. AGSA and Queensland Art Gallery (QAG) acquire her works. Receives Australia Council Visual Arts Board (VAB) project grant and subsequently becomes a Peer Assessor. Elwyn (Jack) Lynn writes on her in *Art International,* and Ray Hughes encourages her to retain the double-barrelled married Lillecrapp-Fuller surname.

1983 ——— 1985 ¶ Exhibits in *Australian Perspecta 1983* at the Art Gallery of New South Wales. In Melbourne, Mary Macqueen encourages her to paint in watercolour. After accompanying Felix Hess to Northern Australia on a sound-recording field trip, moves with him to Groningen in the Netherlands to explore the European art world. Begins painting with oil paints. ¶ Returning to Australia, develops interest in furniture-making while working as graphic and interpretations consultant for Gulf Station National Trust farm at Yarra Glen, Victoria. Returns to Brisbane and shares warehouse with artists in Kangaroo Point. Begins collecting crockery from second-hand shops, which become the subject of watercolour, photographic, collage and sculptural artworks, later shown at Monash University Museum of Art (MUMA), UQ Art Museum and AGSA.

1986 ——— 1988 ¶ Spends three months living in Sri Satchanalai, central Thailand, as a volunteer documentary illustrator for Thai Ceramic Archaeological Project. Moves frequently between Adelaide and Melbourne, and travels again to the Netherlands and United Kingdom. Holds solo and group exhibitions in Brisbane at Ray Hughes Gallery, QAG, Griffith Artworks (now Griffith University Art Museum) and Gold Coast City Gallery (now HOTA, Home of the Arts). ¶ Produces artworks in response to the demolition of many Brisbane inner-city houses, which curator Stephen Rainbird later includes in the exhibition *Cool Quiet Art* at Ipswich Art Gallery, with artists June Tupicoff, Leonard Brown and Madonna Staunton. National Gallery of Australia (NGA) acquires six works, and the new Parliament House in Canberra acquires four watercolours. Awarded a VAB Project grant, and ends her relationship with gallerist Ray Hughes.

Timeline 1980 ——— 1991

1989 ——— 1990 ¶ Becomes full-time painting lecturer at QUT. Travels to Cooper Creek and Lake Killalpaninna in South Australia with Antony Hamilton, and to Bali, Indonesia, for a cultural tour and wood-carving workshop. Begins incorporating colourful pegs, plastics, toothbrushes, Victoria and Albert Museum calendar papers, stitching on linen, and clothes patterns into her work. Holds two solo shows at Savode Gallery, Brisbane, and exhibits in group exhibitions at QUT Art Museum, the Museum of Contemporary Art (MOCA) in Brisbane, Institute of Modern Art (IMA) in Brisbane, and Gold Coast City Gallery. Included in *Shot from Down Under*, an exhibition of nine Australian photographers, held in the Japanese cities of Tokyo, Osaka and Nagoya. Meets the Chinese calligrapher and graphic designer David Zhu, and they marry in Brisbane in 1990.

1991 ¶ A major mid-career survey and touring exhibition, *Helen Lillecrapp-Fuller: A Visual Diary 1979–91,* curated by Stephen Rainbird, opens at QAG when Fuller is eight months pregnant. Participates in the travelling exhibition *Fertile Ground: Contemporary Views of Australian Landscape* at Griffith Artworks, and QAG and QUT acquire her artworks. Fuller and Zhu's son, Alexander Fuller-Zhu, is born 19 September 1991, and Fuller's father passes away on the same day in Adelaide.

Timeline 1980 —— 1991

Helen Fuller, *Fireblanket 1 and 2*, 1980, mixed media construction, 54.8 × 75.6 × 7.6 cm. Griffith University Art Collection. Photograph Carl Warner.

041

Works

Helen Fuller, *Art labels and hang-ups*, 1981, mixed media in four wooden boxes, glass, each box 92.5 x 59.0 cm. Art Gallery of South Australia Collection. Elder Bequest Fund 1981.

Works

Helen Fuller, *Brisbane Still-Life No. 1*, 1986, watercolour, 30.5 x 40.5 cm. Artbank Collection, purchased 1986.

Helen Fuller

Helen Fuller, *Brisbane Still-Life No. 5*, 1986, watercolour, 30.5 x 40.5 cm. Artbank Collection, purchased 1986.

Helen Fuller, *Collected shadows*, 1986, direct positive colour photograph on paper, four panels: 40.6 x 31 cm (each). Queensland Art Gallery | Gallery of Modern Art. Purchased 1992, Queensland Art Gallery Foundation. Photograph Natasha Harth.

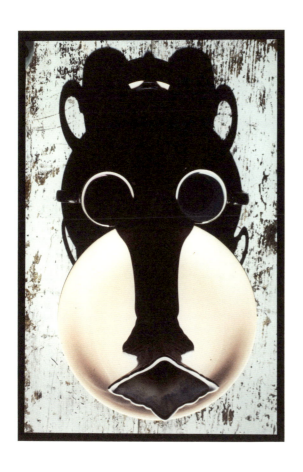

Works

Helen Fuller

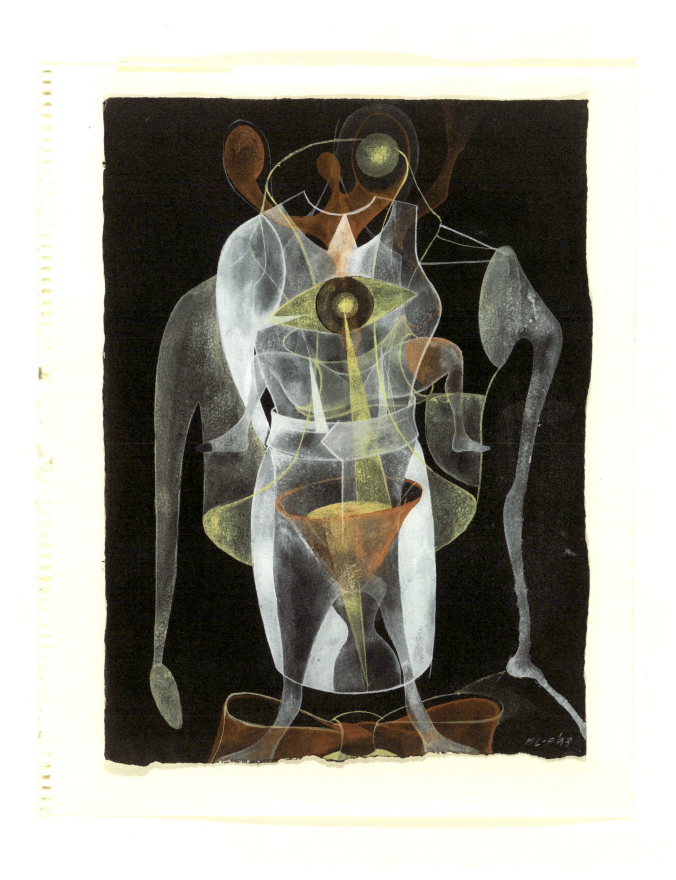

Helen Fuller, *Untitled*, 1993, drawing in gouache, paper,
38.0 x 28.6 cm. National Gallery of Australia Collection, Kamberri/Canberra.

Helen Fuller, *Bower house*, 1990, collage of found objects stitched to the pages of a diary, four stones and text on paper, four panels, 29.5 x 23.4 cm (each). Queensland Art Gallery | Gallery of Modern Art. Purchased 1992, Queensland Art Gallery Foundation. Photograph Natasha Harth.

051

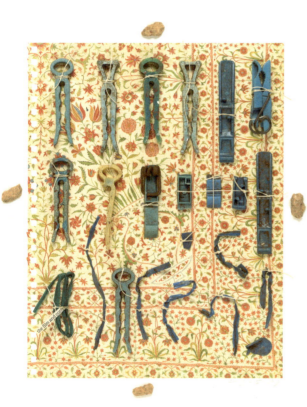 

Works

Helen Fuller, *Pegged Out*, 1990, fragments of plastic clothes pegs on board, 53 x 43 cm. Collection Helen Watters. Photograph Julie Millowick.

Helen Fuller

053

Works

Helen Fuller

Helen Fuller: Making and Un-making Home
essay by Sasha Grbich

As a child, the treasure trove of broken crockery and old bottles Helen dug up at the bottom of her garden made better toys than the dolls she was given to play with. In that suburban Adelaide backyard, she directed an unruly archaeological dig in which stories were the rich seam that ran between her findings.

This writing grew from the wry stories of a kitchen table conversation through which we considered five decades of Helen's work in relation to the material space of the home. It is domestic, and it is personal, she says firmly. Artworks were pulled out and handled, grounding narratives in pigments, oxides and mud. I look up from the table to see a button sewn onto ink-stained Chinese paper overlayed with housepaint in a faltering grid-like pattern that reminds me of the Besser block homes lining Adelaide streets. The marks on nearby clay vessels are imprints from sticks picked up on her daily walks. Each found thing and patterned surface connects loosely to the next, to see how it fits—and to enjoy how it comes apart like pulled stitches. There are no straight lines in her works or in the recounting of them. Her oeuvre is like a brimful house that at each turn elicits greater noticing. Patterns dance in waves across decades as they glean new materials to rest on, or as objects that become assemblages. The story of my art practice is full of flotsam, she observes.

Almost one hundred years ago, Virginia Woolf recounted the progress of her own body through her city, its architectures and institutions, mapping the moments in which her stride, eye, mind or the reach of her tongue were curtailed in their movements.[26] She concludes that with some income, and the privacy of a room of one's own, a woman might create a universe that turns obliquely to the motion of the world outside. Helen was told by her parents that she would never be a real woman if she didn't have a husband and child, and she responded by deciding early in life to not be a woman on those terms. Following Woolf's invitation, Fuller went on to nurture wild, disobedient things in her room, firstly by making collages, assemblages and installations that reconfigured the restrictive domesticity and familial relationships that had walled her in.

Helen Fuller, *Black Sheep + White elephant* detail, 2004, installation view, Prospect Gallery, Adelaide, greaseproof lunch wrap, pins, pegs, cotton wire. Photograph Michal Kluvanek.

Helen recalls growing up on a street where women learnt needlework, knew their role as housekeeper and were housebound. To her, art school looked like a door to leave through. To her parents, it signified sex, drugs and rock and roll—certainly not the place for a decent young lady. Helping her in a manner appropriate to their values, they found her work as a medical illustrator which eventually led to her training for the more socially sanctioned job of teacher. By her mid-twenties she did get married and began teaching high school art. Helen proudly recalls this time as one during which she enacted a series of wilful failures. By her late twenties she had given it all up (first the art teaching, and, soon after, the marriage) and began to put herself through art school.

At art school, at 28 years old, there was sex, drugs and rock and roll (as predicted) but she recalls that women mostly just got to be the sex objects. Helen had few female mentors at that time, but she does recall the quiet strength of one of her teachers, Helen Macintosh, recounting a moment when Macintosh gently held her hand whilst they stood for a photo, providing solidarity amidst a storm of male energy. Helen later painted her an homage when an archive of Helen Macintosh's dried paints was gifted posthumously. She carefully ground the pigments to create undulating grids in pinks and iridescent blues, establishing thereby a connection with her teacher's hands again through time—each echoing the other in the pleasures of mark-making.[27]

Helen Fuller, *Black and white corsets*, 1979, corsets, child's shoes, cotton wadding, white bread, synthetic polymer paint, palette knife, fork, thread, fishing hooks, plastic figurine, 68.0 x 82.3 x 4.5 cm. Collection of The University of Queensland, purchased with the assistance of the Visual Arts Board of the Australia Council, 1979. Photograph Carl Warner.

Helen Fuller, South Australian School of Art Masters and Graduate Diploma exhibition, 1993, installation view, UniSA Art Museum, mixed media. Photograph Michal Kluvanek.

Wilful failure like Helen's is a productive site of alterity where those who refuse to fulfill familial and other normative models of success might create spaces in which to thrive. Helen also speaks about the joy of starting from the failure of purpose inherent in working with discarded things. She recalls trawling the dunes and rubbish dumps on the Yorke Peninsula to make *Moonta objects - Utensils* (1982) and *Sticks and stones* (1982). Bones, household objects, horsehair and a castration ring (amongst other findings) are formed into assertive, messy bodies that look a little like creatures, more like cutlery, and seem to pose a suggestive invitation to the mouth.[28]

H. J. Johnstone's *Evening shadows, backwater of the Murray, South Australia* (1880) holds dominance in local art historical imagination as the first acquisition of the Art Gallery of South Australia. Bucking familial expectations that she might turn the whole messy art school experience towards a career as a landscape painter, Helen instead targeted that genteel construction of place. In her version, titled *School teacher of fish said yes that looks very good* (1981), dried fish bodies line up in shadow boxes. Those animals invisible in the original painting are brought to the surface in a manner that calls attention to the deaths implicit in museumification and that also questions institutional knowledge. This assemblage is rotting somewhere in a public collection in Queensland, where, stinking up an archive, it provides a satisfyingly irreverent response not only to Johnstone's painting but also to its prime position in the formation and perpetuation of institutions.

Helen Fuller: Making and Un-making Home

The house is a body that structures communities by holding hierarchies in place, setting structures in place using bricks and stones. The naming of the master bedroom reveals its dominance, the kitchen table is a feminised place to work and chat, and down that spine of a corridor are some smaller spaces where those less powerful children can be found. Helen's reconfiguration of domesticity includes a decisive archaeology of the nuclear family she was born into. After her father died, she made the installation *BCF* (1995) with the entire contents of his shed. Amidst that exquisite one-person museum, two filing cabinets stood facing each other as if at high noon, their drawers held together such that if you were to pull out one, the other would recede in an eternally unresolved stand-off. That's me and my father gnashing our teeth, she says.

Later turning her gaze to her mother, in *Penance* (2004) Helen observed her unquestioning acceptance of a life formed around four children, the Church and her plodding un-aesthetic Methodist-ness. A collection of rags pulled through a wooden picnic table draws a confident cross on its surface and dangles below. Underneath, reflected in an ornate mirror lain on the floor, an anarchic under-space opens where rigid Christian ontology gives way. It is bit like looking up the skirt of a nun. The work is redolent with sacrilegious humour and is a prescient example of Helen's ability to inhabit structures in her own way by articulating imaginative worlds just below the veneer of respectability.

But what of the children? What are they up to, hidden from view in those rooms down the corridor? *I don't know what to do if she draws red horses and red men all the time* (1979) is a lament that runs through a series of 17 works, one created for each word. Stamped onto each image's surfaces are the words 'zoo', '1979' and 'Amsterdam', making this series of anti-postcards, each centred on the same photograph of a mother turning away, leaving an ambiguous event between three children in focus. Every iteration is hand-coloured differently, as if a code is being deciphered or revealed. Limp balloons sandwiched into the frame at mouth level might reveal an absurd morse code if inflated. Irrationality and disorder have become guiding principles, celebrating the wilful refusal that children can wield.

Helen Fuller, *PAINT rags*, 2006, commissioned for In the World: head, hand, heart, 17th Tamworth Fibre Textile Biennial, 2006, plastic baskets, recycled rags, polyester ribbon, safety pins. Photograph Michal Kluvanek.

Helen preferred her grandparents' house. It was there that she encountered the subversive potential of craft, and fondly remembers her grandmother heading to Country Women's Association meetings, which she understood to be an escape from domestic entombment, albeit one complicit in the maintenance of that perpetual state. She recounts the story of packets of mixed canary seed emptied onto the table for her to sort into colours and tones which her grandmother then glued into typical colonial landscape scenes. Terrible images, she says, like an Aboriginal man standing on one leg looking at the sunset. She found herself amidst a complex problem with craft practices both perpetuating colonial images and also being a space for expression of marginalised female subjectivities. Helen responded by taking up the potential of the kitchen table as site for un-making expectations of domesticity or, as Rozsika Parker theorises, using subversive stitches to unpick entrenched roles and representations.[29]

Sasha Grbich

Helen's earliest exhibitions were being held as the politics of the home swung into focus with the women's movement's position that 'the personal is political' making visible and powerful the conditions of women's domestic lives.[30] In 1975, feminism in Adelaide was catalysed when American art theorist Lucy Lippard visited the Adelaide chapter of the Women's Art Movement (WAM).[31] Although WAM created local opportunities and visibility for women artists, Helen didn't become directly involved with its programs and meetings, describing herself as its quiet outsider. Nonetheless, at that time she too made works that brought forward restrictions on women's lives and bodies, her 1979 installation *Course it's Art* responding to a memory of her Grandma Knox and the corset that trussed her flesh. The work caught the moment of flight when restrictive clothing was thrown off and satisfied scratching would follow the unhooking of the thing, to get blood back into all the crevices. In the gallery, the heavy bat-like undergarments were painted thickly with colour and pinned to the wall like a flock, their tactile surfaces holding the memories of women's bodies and activity.

Leaving home, Helen moved to Brisbane in the early 1980s to take up the opportunity to show with Ray Hughes Gallery. She stayed for more than a decade and found the city looser and more accommodating. She learnt to drink beer and remembers Davida Allen's work for the freedom that danced off her sexy, mouthy images. Helen went up to Queensland to show collages that soon became densely patterned painted works, continuing into two dimensions the irreverence of earlier salvaged installations and assemblages. Soon after moving north, she began teaching painting at Queensland University of Technology.

I'm a serial killer, she says. We are in her studio, and she is referring to thick piles of papers on deep stacked shelves across which patterns repeat and change. Each nuanced surface is won through rigorous rearrangement of line, colour, shape and materials that shift continuously under the direction of a playful eye. The austere geometries of hard-edged abstraction and the industrial fabrication methods of minimalism are thoroughly mocked by her confidently shaky hand-drawn lines and pleasurable material excesses. Discussions of feminist art practices from the 1970s forward have most often attended to representational works, with asserting visibility of women's bodies and stories a key political strategy.[32] Against this tendency, in Helen's hands, abstraction becomes an open space for continuous reinvention and exploration of female subjectivity through tactility, and with humour.

From her early years in Adelaide, Helen remembers the straight lines and hard edges of Sydney Ball (who she recalls returning from America, masking tape in hand) and being drawn to Virginia Jay's work for its concentric echoing circles. But it was in Brisbane where she found approaches more in keeping with her own, locating more comfortably between the gentle approaches to mark-making and colour being taught by William Robinson (her colleague at QUT) and the energetic, gestural marks, spills and layers she observed in the works of Robert Moore and Joe Furlonger. In her own reckoning with formalism, layered grids are set up with faltering lines that escape their more rigid historical origins. Dressmaking methods like tacking and unpicking, along with references to the weave and repetition of fabric patterns, bring her approach to abstraction into continuous relation with the materiality of the home. There are momentary flips into representation: for example, when a broken egg joyfully makes messy the conventions of abstract space, as if accidentally smashing onto a tabletop.

Helen Fuller, *Penance*, 2004, installation detail, Ephemeral to the Eternal exhibition, UniSA Art Museum, white cotton industrial rags, timber slats and mirror, plastic buckets. Photograph Helen Fuller.

Lucy Lippard's term 'eccentric abstraction' sits most comfortably with Helen's approach. Writing in 1966, Lippard observed artists learning from (and rejecting) the formalism preceding them through discussions of the abstract sculptural works of Eva Hesse and Louise Bourgeois, noting their perverse, humorous and irreverent approaches.[33] What Helen shares is the staking out of a space that is neither figurative nor formalist but where sensorial patterns and materials playfully proliferate. Helen's thread within this history is nuanced by its proximity to the decorative arts, perhaps flavoured by her emergence in a city where Margaret Preston's works were being rediscovered and Barbara Hanrahan's prints, pulsating with surface detail, were being shown.

Helen's *Table Map* (2009) is testament to her ability to playfully adapt the aesthetics of domesticity into open-ended surface-heavy paintings. It is from a series made in gouache, ink and collage on paper crossed by lines running so close to one another as to evoke the fine mesh of gauze, overmarked thickly like a map. The paintings seem to follow the breath of a table as it repeatedly fills and empties again, marking the passing of plates, the leaving of stains, and chairs pushed out and tidied in. Helen recalled Daniel Spoerri's *tableaux pièges*, formed when the artist would call a halt mid-dinner party and fastidiously glue down and exhibit the table surface. Where Spoerri's tabletops make resonant a moment, Helen's have the tender-worn quality of a collection of stains and repairs that communicate a lifetime of daily washing and cooking.

Not long after Helen left Brisbane, Davida Allen began working on her film *Feeling Sexy* (1999), telling the story of a woman artist (played by Susie Porter) who is a painter struggling within the isolating conventions of marriage and motherhood. After years of travelling between Melbourne, China and Brisbane, Helen returned to Adelaide in her forties with her newborn son, Alex. It changed things for her. Things go differently when you turn up to your own interstate exhibition with a baby on your hip, she says—they take you straight to the hotel and they leave you there.

Linda Nochlin, in reply to her own provocative question as to why there have been no great women artists, identifies problems associated with structuring women into the domestic sphere separated from male-dominated arenas of cultural production.[34] Helen's long practice contributes to this provocation by thoroughly examining the control and freedom possible in domestic spaces. The second half of her story follows her reformation of the home as a shelter for creative production where decorative objects with excessively patterned surfaces are produced with rapacious speed. Writing about houses in the work of surrealists, Jane Alison observes their excesses in collecting, making and display as a kind of surreal ecstasy in an overload of information, which stands guard against the rationality of modernism.[35] Helen adds pleasure to this equation. Her excessive use of pattern on paper and clay surfaces is a tornado of ornamentation that has carried her career through masculinist traditions in abstraction as well as Adelaide's male-dominated conceptual art movement.[36] Rather than finding a way into masculine arenas (as Nochlin anticipates), Helen has shifted the site of cultural production by taking it home with her.

It is very tucked-in around here, she observes, looking out from her front gate. A free settlement of liberal, religious non-conformists, Adelaide was nonetheless designed on the premise of a traditional family structure with its particularly moral fervour rooted in differentiating itself from the evils of neighbouring penal colonies.[37] A culture of tucking away the wayward followed early libertarian leanings wherein public control coexisted with private freedom. Here rebellion incubates and emanates from inside houses, as Helen's has.

Sasha Grbich

Helen admires the artist Louise Bourgeois for her vitality and unconventionality. Both are artists of entangled domestic returns, a life-long concern explored finally in Bourgeois's *Cells*, where caged domains locate reworked domestic memories furnished with part bodies and tapestries. Fuller's reckoning with the domestic includes many returns to Adelaide, where her making is now inseparable from the dense jungle of things she finds and coinhabits with. After decades, it is not clear if walls hold up the artworks or the artworks support the walls. I like to imagine the latter, that is that her artworks have broken the house and are making a dwelling anew from the ruin of domesticity past, oscillating as Helen does between the poles of making and unmaking home. The character of her in-dwelling is nicely echoed in Walter Benjamin's observation that amidst cosy collecting there is the possibility to hold oneself as if spider in web, secluded in a heady dream amidst spoils from the world.[38] Helen might prefer Bourgeois's spider towering over one of her *Cells* in a wonderful image of motherhood as safe when sheltered beneath and terrifying to confront.

In her house, the story of Helen's practice can be followed transversally along strata of patterning and arranging. Surfaces developed years apart find themselves in unexpected relation, with her handmade vessels the siblings/ancestors of the paintings. Helen's ceramics evoke something of the residual escape of the shadowy other-land of Maurice Sendak's wonderful children's book *Where the Wild Things Are* (1963), its monsters first blossoming as shapes on walls. In her hands, that wild potential is rekindled as a constellation of vessels which, when caught in the corner of my view, become beak-like and beady-eyed. Their liveliness rumbles under their joyfully decorated clay surfaces, erupting now and then with the irreverence of kookaburra laughter. Looping back again through time, they might be in cahoots with photographs that form the series *Collected shadows* (1992), where arrangements of commercially made cups and plates are positioned to reveal the ghosts of impertinent creatures, open-mouthed and gleeful.

Helen Fuller, *Mutant Paradigm*, 1997, installation view, Contemporary Art Centre South Australia. Photograph Michal Kluvanek.

The terracotta clay Helen uses is dug from the earth in Magill, not so far from that first backyard where she excavated her early playthings. Terracotta is the butcher's paper of clays, she says. And recalling her love of working with materials from around the home, she reminds me of earlier work *Frock* (2004), where a carefully made baby's christening dress is formed using kitchen baking paper. Ever funny and fierce, the arms of the little dress are elongated and rolled up to form toilet-paper-roll-like little clenched fists. Rather than show the object itself, Helen chose to exhibit two photographs, identical but with the tones inverted so that the ceremonial dress cohabits with its darker flipside. They seem an appropriate monument to a lifetime of strong-willed resistance delivered with great humour and threaded thickly with material pleasure.

—— **Sasha Grbich**

26 Virginia Woolfe, *A Room of One's Own* (Penguin, Random House: UK, 2019. First published Hogarth Press, 1928).

27 While this story is here told through conversation with the artist, an account of this story is beautifully written by Cath Kenneally in her article 'Domestic Forensics'. https://www.artlink.com.au/articles/3137/helen-fuller-domestic-forensics/, accessed September 2022.

28 This detailed list of materials is drawn from exhibition catalogue Stephen Rainbird, *Helen Lillecrapp-Fuller: A Visual Diary 1979–91* (Queensland University of Technology, 1991), p5.

29 Rozsika Parker, *The Subversive Stitch: Embroidery and the Making of the Feminine* (Women's Press: London, 1984).

30 Catherine Speck and Catriona Moore, 'How the personal became (and remains) political in the visual arts', in Michelle Arrow and Angela Woollacott (eds), *Everyday Revolutions: Remaking Gender, Sexuality and Culture in 1970s Australia* (ANU Press, 2019).

31 American feminist art theorist Lucy Lippard was brought to Australia by the Power Institute, University of Sydney, to deliver the Power Lecture in major Australian cities in 1975. The history of Adelaide's WAM can be found at http://www.womenaustralia.info/biogs/AWE1034b.htm, accessed November 2022.

32 This follows assertions made by Susan L. Stoops in her introduction to the exhibition catalogue *More Than Minimal: Feminism and Abstraction in the 70s* (Rose Art Museum, Brandeis University: Waltham, MA, 1996) p6.

33 *Eccentric Abstraction* (first published in 1966) is included in Lucy R. Lippard, *Changing Essays in Art Criticism* (Dutton and Co: New York, 1971).

34 Linda Nochlin, 'Why Have There Been No Great Women Artists?', in *Women, Art and Power*, ed. Linda Nochlin (Harper and Row: New York, 1988), p150.

35 Jane Alison, *The Surreal House* (Barbican Art Gallery, Yale University Press: New Haven and London, 2010), p40.

36 My current PhD research tracks gender inequality in the formation of experimental art histories in Adelaide 1974–1984.

37 Dino Hodge, *Don Dunstan, Intimacy and Liberty: A political biography* (Wakefield Press: Adelaide, 2014), p21.

38 Walter Benjamin, *The Arcades Project* (The Belknap Press of Harvard University Press: Cambridge, Massachusetts and London, 1982), p216.

Sasha Grbich

1992

Helen Fuller

2008

Timeline 1992 —— 2008

1992 ——— 1993 ¶ Returns to Adelaide with her new family and commences a Master of Visual Arts at SASA, University of South Australia, sharing a studio with artists Angela Valamanesh and Paul Hoban, and working as a casual (Honours) lecturer at SASA. Her exhibition *A Visual Diary* tours regionally in Queensland, and Beth Jackson writes on her in *Eyeline* magazine. Fuller becomes the inaugural recipient of an Asialink Artist-in-Residency at Zhejiang Academy of Fine Arts, Hangzhou, China. Zhu and her son accompany her on the residency. Begins working with Chinese rice paper. Reclaims her family name, and holds solo exhibition at the China World Hotel in Beijing as Helen Fuller.

1994 ¶ Graduates from SASA with a Master of Visual Arts. Presents solo exhibition of recent drawings at Helen Maxwell's Australian Girls Own Gallery (aGOG) in Canberra.

1995 ——— 1997 ¶ Presents a major installation—*Helen Fuller: BCF*—at University of South Australia Art Museum (Underdale), curated by Erica Green, and with a catalogue essay by Ruth Fazakerley. John Neylon subsequently writes catalogue essay for the spinoff exhibition, *BCF: Caravan*, at Australian Experimental Art Foundation (AEAF). Awarded two Arts SA project grants. Solo exhibitions of drawings at aGOG and Joe Airo-Farulla's Gallery 482 in Brisbane. Participates in group shows at AGSA, QAG, Contemporary Art Centre of South Australia (CACSA) and Adelaide Festival Artists' Week. NGA acquires four of her *Spleen* series drawings. Contributes tribute to her father's shed, 'Planed All Around', in *Stories From The Shed*, edited by Mark Thomson.

Helen Fuller

1998 ¶ Accompanied by her 80-year-old mother and six-year-old son, Fuller undertakes an artist-in-residence project at Queensland's Noosa Regional Gallery, and upscales the contents of grandmother Maude's button tin for a solo exhibition, *Buttons,* at Gallery 482. Participates in two, two-person shows—one with Ian North at Experimental Art Foundation and the other with Annette McKee at JamFactory in Adelaide. Participates in *All this and Heaven too*, Juliana Engberg and Ewan McDonald's *Adelaide Biennale of Australian Art* at AGSA.

1999 ——— 2000 ¶ Continues to deconstruct her familial ties and to play with words and conventions in her *D press* performances for Nexus Gallery's *Public Studio Project,* publicly ironing clothes outside David Jones department store in Adelaide's Rundle Mall and gifting them to homeless passers-by, and in the exhibition *White Shed*, with Alison Main and Nikki Vouis, at CACSA. Writes on Julie Blyfield for Gray St (jewellery) Workshop's *Celebrating 15 years* anthology. Participates in AGSA exhibition *Chemistry,* curated by Sarah Thomas. Fuller's mother passes away on 6 September 2000.

2001 ——— 2003 ¶ Continues her exploration of fabrics as subject in *Installation Stills* at CACSA and Centre for Contemporary Photography (CCP), Melbourne, as well as in *Home Is Where the Heart Is,* a touring exhibition combining works from contemporary artists and Country Women's Association members, curated by Vivonne Thwaites. ¶ Works as artist-in-residence at Adelaide's Wilderness School, involving a collaborative installation by art staff and students: a four-metre-diameter floral mandala using fresh-cut flowers, fruits and gathered leaves, recalling the North Terrace Flower Day exhibitions of her childhood. A second outcome is *Happy Days,* made for the babies born to unmarried girls at McBride's Hospital opposite the school. After twelve years, Fuller ceases lecturing at SASA.

Timeline 1992 —— 2008

2004 ¶ Fuller's eldest brother, civil engineer Trevor, retires and opens the Watson Place Gallery in Flinders Lane, Melbourne, which later moves to Richmond as Place Gallery. He presents his sister's solo show *Dirndl Patterns,* with a catalogue essay by Caroline Philipp. Fuller's artwork shown in *Fragments* at QAG and *Universal Playground* at Stephen Page's *Adelaide Festival.* ¶ Contributes her work *Penance* to the exhibition *From the Ephemeral to the Eternal*, with Eugene Carchesio and Madonna Staunton, at the UniSA Art Museum, which continues her scrutiny of remembered domestic duty, and being 'on the rags' as a teenager. *White Elephant Black Sheep* at Prospect Gallery in Adelaide, with a catalogue essay by Judith Green, surveys her ties to grandmother Maude. Awarded an Arts SA professional development grant, and mentors Laura Wills.

2005 ——— 2006 ¶ During further travels to China, makes new artworks on rice paper gifted to her by David's brother Christopher, deputy director at the Shanghai Museum. Participates in exhibitions at Sullivan+Strumpf Fine Art, Sydney, and at Place Gallery, Melbourne. The exhibition *Dirndl Grids,* now at Helen Maxwell Gallery, ACT, is reviewed by art historian Sasha Grishin. Continues experimenting with oil on canvas boards, still life and geometric patterns, many of which are later destroyed. A lively cycle of exhibiting, including *National Works on Paper*, Mornington Peninsula Regional Gallery, *17th Fibre Textile Biennial*, Tamworth, and *Moist: Australian Watercolours* at the NGA and touring nationally. Features new works in *Writing a painting* with Robin Best, Nyukana (Daisy) Baker and Huang Xiuqian, curated by Vivonne Thwaites, an exhibition to launch the University of South Australia's SASA Gallery at City West campus. With catalogue essays by Nicholas Jose and Mary Eagle.

2007 ——— 2008 ¶ An artist residency at the Australian Tapestry Workshop in Melbourne results in *Sampler*, a solo exhibition of small paintings on torn corrugated cardboard. Exhibits with Sandy Naulty in *An anthology of significant finds* at Red Poles, McLaren Vale. After accompanying her friend Julie Blyfield to her Paris exhibition and revisiting Amsterdam, creates blue and white works which visualise the intimacy of air, breath, condensation and ice crystals, which then become the exhibition *VAPOUR* at Sullivan+Strumpf, Sydney. Awarded an Arts SA special project grant. 'Domestic Forensics' by Cath Kenneally, written for *Artlink* magazine, records Fuller's first experiments with handmade clay pots. The weaver Cheryl Thornton weaves four small Fuller watercolours in *Post* at Place Gallery.

Helen Fuller, *Buttons No. 1, 3, 4, 5, 12, 23*, 1998, paint, wood, paper labels, button diameters left to right: 12.5, 12, 13, 12, 12 & 14 cm. Cruthers Collection of Women's Art, The University of Western Australia.

Helen Fuller

Works

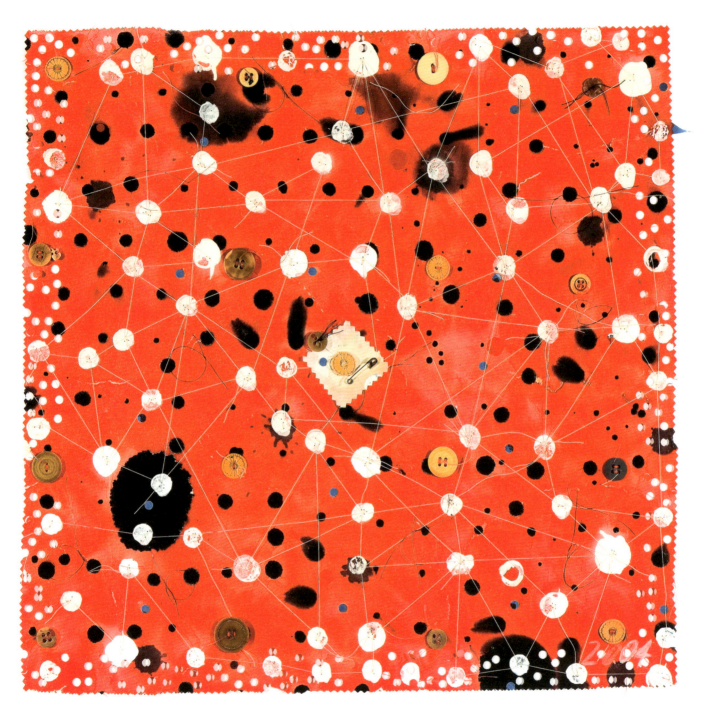

Helen Fuller, *Cushion II*, 2003, acrylic and mixed media, 67.5 x 72 cm.
Cruthers Collection of Women's Art, The University of Western Australia.

Helen Fuller

Helen Fuller, *Cushion I*, 2003, acrylic and mixed media, 67.5 x 72 cm. Cruthers Collection of Women's Art, The University of Western Australia.

Helen Fuller, *Wallflower*, 2001, installation view, *Home is Where the Heart Is* touring exhibition, brown paper, lunch wrap, wire, cotton. Photograph Michal Kluvanek.

Helen Fuller

Works

Helen Fuller

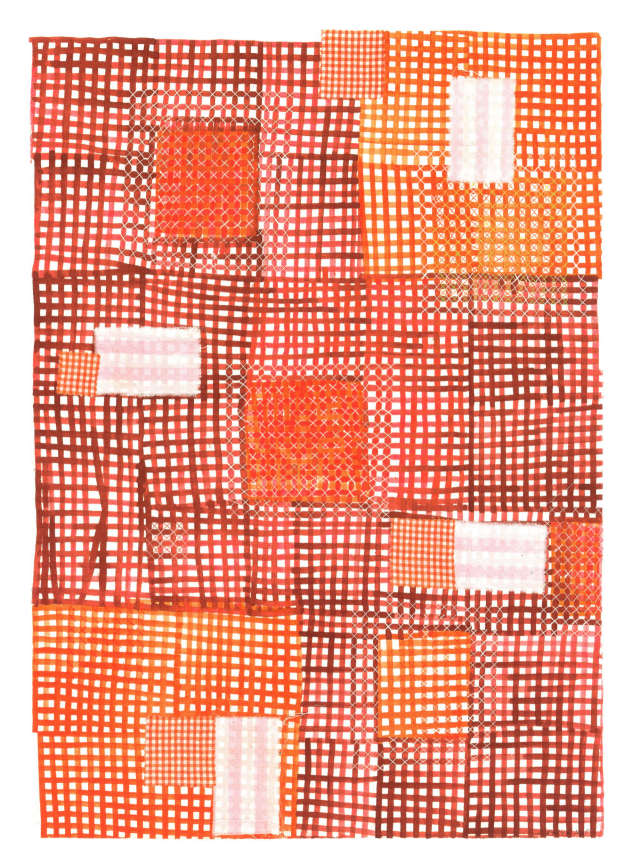

Helen Fuller, *Blood orange*, 2005, collage of gingham and cotton with additions in gouache, thick white Waterford paper, 76.6 x 55.4 cm. National Gallery of Australia Collection, Kamberri/Canberra.

Helen Fuller

Helen Fuller, *BCF*, 1995, installation view, UniSA Art Museum, mixed media. Photograph Michal Kluvanek.

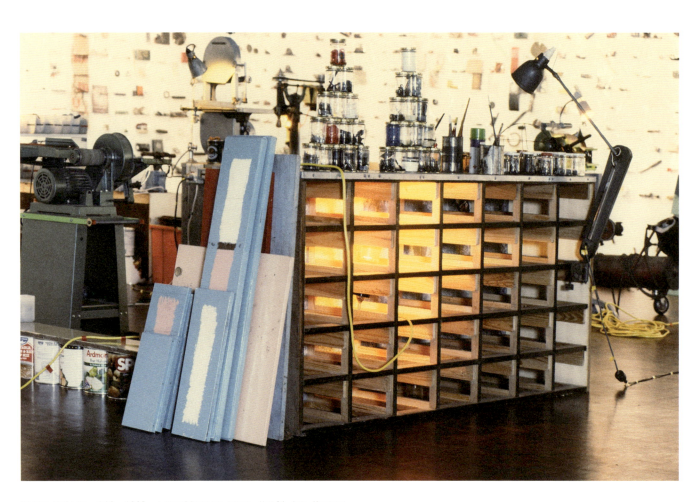

Helen Fuller, *BCF*, 1995, installation view, UniSA Art Museum, mixed media. Photograph Michal Kluvanek.

Helen Fuller

Works

 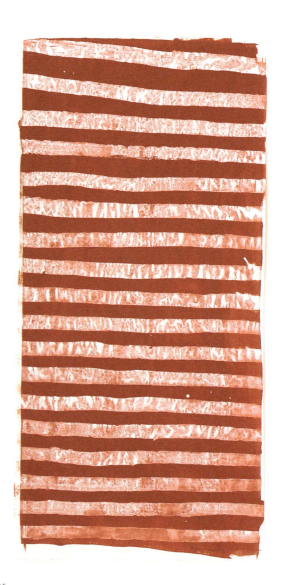

Helen Fuller, selected works from the series *Rag Trade*, 2005, acrylic on Chinese paper, each work, 99 x 50 cm. Various collections. Photograph Michal Kluvanek.

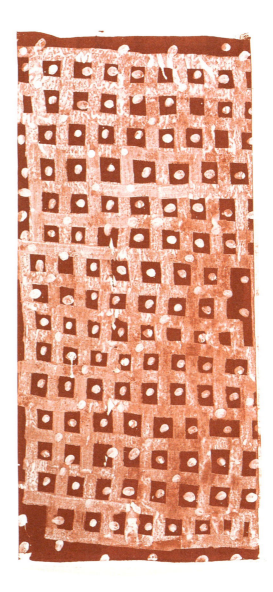

Helen Fuller

Knowledge may have its purposes, but guessing is always more fun than knowing.

'Archaeology', WH Auden

Helen Fuller: Pots
essay by Glenn Barkley

Hand-building is the place where many people start to work with ceramics. It is where kids usually begin their pottery journey, making lumpen forms that draw out ceramics' immediacy and gestural potential. Countless workshops for beginners' hand-building have blossomed across the country in the last ten years, and vast making empires, access studios and overpriced mail-order DIY ceramic kits have been built on the simple premise that ceramics is not the internet. The last few years of lockdowns have only amplified hand-making as the method *du jour* of ceramics

Unlike the implied intensity of the thrown pot—all that purity, all that centring, and, really, who has the time?—hand-building has an immediacy that's hard to beat. Tactile and scatological, it taps into a primal, lizard brain and unlocks a sense of touch and wonder. An object being poorly made—sagging, folding and collapsing under its own weight—can be a virtue rather than something heading straight to the slops bucket. Simply open the bag, stick in your hand and away you go. No need for endless wedging—you can even make it in your kitchen or your toilet.

And where throwing can appear cultish and religious, with its own wise (mainly) male sages and gatekeepers, hand-building is the open, broken doorway that can truly claim to be the blues—or the punk rock—of the pottery world. Both these musical styles have immediacy at the core; they foreground emotion over proficiency, although that does mean you can approach a cobbled-together kind of virtuosity that, when done properly, still maintains its rough edges. Both can accommodate the untaught and marginal as well as the skilful and knowing. They can be made simply, with simple equipment, and, like hand-building, both musical forms are initially easy to learn but extremely difficult to master. It's easy—and immediately compelling—to make a sound but it's hard to turn that into a song, and quite addictive.

I start with this because Helen Fuller began making pots in 2009 and her work is determinedly and resolutely hand-built. Like many contemporary ceramicists, Fuller's ceramics are also the outcome of, or adjacent to, a second artistic career.[39] Her now accomplished and celebrated body of work as a ceramicist began at a hobby level, joining a class where she may have been seen and considered somewhat of an outsider. Less interested in the practicalities of ceramics, she was instantly drawn to its informal aspects and its ambiguities. She felt a bit of a failure, and her work went through a rapid period of building and destruction, Fuller often chucking pots sheepishly in the bin on the way home from the classroom.[40]

Helen Fuller, *Jug*, 2014, hand-built white raku clay, porcelain slip, black oxide. Collection Ingrid Kellenbach. Photograph Michael Field.

Fuller's pots have many precedents and parents, and Fuller seems to be a very knowing kind of maker as well as a very painterly one. The pots sometimes resemble vessels you might find in a cubist still life that have now miraculously appeared in three dimensions—useless flat handles, angled spouts to nowhere, slip decoration that sometimes delineates shapes and at other times describes a shape both as profile and as negative. Surfaces are embossed and then painted over. Holes are excavated. Surfaces are dimpled and rubbed smooth.

In Fuller's work, painting and drawing and ceramics are intrinsically linked. As a painter, over time her paintings seem to be pushing more and more beyond the formalities of the grid into the realms of the weave, resembling not the gridded austerity of modernism but rather domestic realms—tablecloths, tea towels and cheap gingham dresses—and the minutiae of the natural worlds of cobwebs as well as nature's grandness, like ink-blotted descriptions of celestial skies.[41]

Hand-building can be the most gestural and intuitive way of making pots that has similarity to the tenuous scratchy lines of Fuller's paintings and drawings. The gingham pattern of her paintings has a certain kind of gritty touch, however, that sees them stranded between painting and cloth in the same way her vessels are also caught between painting and ceramic. Like many ceramicists, Fuller finds that the pot or vessel—both its flatness *and* its volume—offers a new surface to decorate that has distinct advantages over a flat canvas. A vessel can be seen in the round—it may have no fixed front or back, or it could have both simultaneously.

Perhaps the space between media is the perfect place for pottery—neither and/or but many things—implying function but not quite functional. For someone coming from painting, the 'not-quite' aspect is probably the thing that draws you to ceramics. Fuller's pots never quite get to the realm of sculpture, which, for the most part, is just that: sculptural, unfunctional, useless, even a bit boring and fixed. Fuller described to me the idea she has that the works retain the essential relationship to the vessels due to the hollow space inside them—a simple, beautiful idea and image that foregrounds the interiors, mostly unseen, as defining the work's essential characteristics.[42]

Vessels, on the other hand, presuppose some use, and that is interesting—a mental and material conundrum you can roll over in your head, and one which gives you a fixed destination from which to deviate. It means you can play with the language of the vessel, a language that is for the most part already fixed and—it must be said—so known to hand and eye as to be rendered simple: here is my handle, here is my spout; this is a foot and this is an aperture; this is the inside and this is the outside. This also applies to the works' scale; they can be small, but they are never monumental. Instead they have a relationship to the tips of the fingers, the hand, the elbow and the shoulder, rather than the whole of the body. This in turn brings them back to the realms of the domestic; they can be picked up and easily handled, brought together, and—in the case of the artist's house and studio— accumulated amongst a lifetime of collection of other objects.

To enclose them would make them sculpture, but by always keeping them open they walk the ambiguous line between vessel and painting—an edge that is compelling to many makers, especially those who have side-shifted over from another visual medium. It is specifically pertinent to Fuller, whose paintings often take another medium or material, another type of flat cloth surface, then loop back to reproducing cloth pattern overlays onto ceramic forms—an endless looping of colour, imagery, surface, pattern and ideas. Some works resemble woven baskets but sit rigid and brittle against the wall—a form of visual trickery making something soft and pliable a painting in a hard, rounded form.

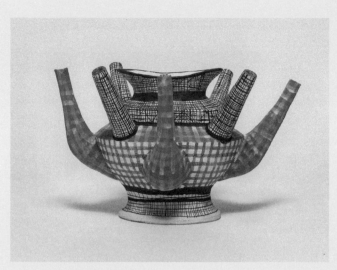

Helen Fuller, *Dutch tulip vase*, 2016, white raku clay with underglaze, oxide, 21 x 35 x 15 cm. Queensland University of Technology Art Collection. Donated by Alan Rix 2018. Photograph Louis Lim.

Fuller's lack of training as a potter holds her in good stead. You may start at one point and just let yourself end up at another. Fuller makes and learns by just doing—sitting down and getting to work. The material will determine its pathway and repetitive acts. Trusted forms—in her case, small bowls made, and designed to be held, in the hand—act to trigger muscle memory. There's nothing like busy hands to kick-start ideas. It also eliminates the idea of being stuck: you just act and do. Often this is about the simple process of letting go, allowing the clay itself to create its own direction. Alternatively, at other times that process is frustrated, and when it does just what you want it to do, this is yet another form of frustration and another obstacle to overcome.

Holding things at the point of collapse—that's the point where you want to be, and, once fired, even the mistakes have a monumental permanence. Fuller's way of making is intensely active, done in a way she has described as 'grow and flow'.[43] Approaching the clay with only the vaguest idea of what it might be, she pushes together coils and pinches and flattens the vessel's walls.

Importantly, she uses Bennetts clay, which is a *lingua franca* of Adelaide ceramics[44]—a fundamental creative and building material. Unlike many other clays, it has few additives and is, for the most part, a single-origin clay body that is sourced locally. Being only a few steps from the producer to the maker, part of its appeal—apart from its distinctive buttery workability that the artist describes as a 'weird soapy feeling'[45]—is that it links those artists that choose to use it with the natural world itself. The artist acknowledges the importance of working with a material close to the source—dug out of a pit north of Adelaide, on Kaurna country, and literally delivered directly to the artist's door. This is a romantic ideal that cleaves nicely with the 20th century Leach-ian ideal of the 'honest potter', but here commercially and geographically achievable. Critically, in the middle of a climate crisis, it's probably a good idea to think more consciously about where your materials come from, and the resources used in their production and distribution.

Bennetts clay symbolically touches upon another important aspect of Fuller's work, that being her part in Adelaide's artistic ecosystem. Whilst not a large city, Adelaide is well-supported by several art schools, public galleries and the national flagship craft institution, JamFactory. The city's small scale also heightens the influence that the Art Gallery of South Australia (AGSA) and its cross-media, cross-cultural thematic displays—especially in regards to the AGSA collection galleries where media, time and materials are mixed in a dynamic melange—may have on makers. To me, as an outside observer, these influences actually feel like they shape Adelaide's very particular artistic impulse, which is far more porous than other capitals, specifically in regards to the way art and craft seem to be superfluous categories.

Helen and Khai Liew, Tarntanya/Adelaide, South Australia, 2022. Photograph Grant Hancock.

Glenn Barkley

Helen Fuller, *Pot [from the series Bark cloth]*, 2011, white raku clay with underglaze decoration, porcelain slip, 20.0 x 34.0 x 31.0 cm. Art Gallery of South Australia Collection. Gift of the artist, 2012.

The roles that JamFactory and AGSA have in encouraging cross-disciplinary approaches means that an artist like Fuller is, although unique and singular, a quintessential Adelaide artist. In her work you can see the conversational relationships between her and jeweller Julie Blyfield—the similar use of marked repoussage or chased surfaces. Sometimes pots are decorated using slip provided by ceramicist Kirsten Coelho, with whom Fuller also shares a sense of scale. The works have the same sense of terroir as those by many of the First Nation Western Desert artists who live and work in the city, including artists from the APY Lands such as Alfred Lowe and Rupert Jack, who both make unglazed ceramics. Fuller's aforementioned collaboration with Khai Liew could also only happen in Adelaide. Lastly, her long friendship with Antony Hamilton, whose disciplined and stark lifestyle stands in contrast to Fuller's urbane one, gives the example of the whittling-down of materials to basic principles and a faith in objects.

Similarly, it is important to note Fuller's earlier work on archaeological sites in Thailand's Ban Ko Noi in 1986—illustrating finds, often fragmentary, focusing on the shapes and patterns as part of a whole or as a thing unto themselves—as an activity that also grew out of Adelaide's dynamic cross-disciplinary cultural community. Fuller, like others (and I would include myself in this group), has spent a long time looking at ceramics. For myself, this has been as curator but for Fuller it was this period in Thailand illustrating these pots. I think that the shape, curves, structure and decoration can't help but imprint themselves in the mind once you have undertaken this kind of sustained looking. And while Fuller herself tends to treat her early works in ceramic as amateurish, they are still very deeply informed. To go from looking to making is a simple step, if you're willing to take it.[46]

Helen Fuller, 2018, hand-built terracotta with underglaze, oxide, porcelain slip. Private Collection. Photograph Grant Hancock.

This period of working also connects Fuller to other pots of the past, and she has spoken of her admiration of Japanese Jōmon pottery. Named after the Japanese word for 'cord', as often cord was impressed into the wet clay, Jōmon pottery maintains an air of power and mystery. More than likely functional, the pots are covered in pattern and design but often shaped like fish bones or fins with looming fanciful tops and apertures. They are about the natural world but also feel a part of it, like the carapace of a great insect or a used seed pod having now become a vessel or container. Importantly, they are not glazed—sometimes only coloured by the low-temperature carbonised atmosphere in which they are fired. Like Fuller, the artists who made them—if we can call them artists—found more than enough in the colour and texture of the clay body itself.

To walk is by a thought to go;
To move in spirit to and fro;
To mind the good we see;
To taste the sweet;
Observing all the things we meet
How choice and rich they be.

'Walking', Thomas Traherne

When I was a kid out walking, I used to snap off the thin spindly stalks of a she-oak, *Casuarina equisetifolia*, and then break the segments down with the tips of my fingers, something I still find deeply reassuring, and still often do when I'm seeing my parents, visiting the town where I grew up, where I feel like I'm skimming across the surface of the past.

The meandering walk, the unconscious ramble as a place to lose oneself, to be comforted, is something that I imagine, like me, is integral to Fuller's work. To Fuller, the pragmatic act of walking the dog turns the mind into a ripe laboratory—*To walk abroad is, not with eyes, / But thoughts*[47]—, stopping to look at plants, finding leaves and seeds, imagining them as stamps or patterns dispersed across the surface of a vessel, looking at the sky, looking at the leaves—all that blue, grey and green.[48]

From these walks Fuller has amassed studio detritus that is harder and harder for her to discard: a humble piece of bark caught peeling from the trunk and branch of a eucalypt; the Banksia serrata leaves that look as though cut with a pair of pinking shears; the dark, popping, crinkly banksia flower pods, redolent and inescapably linked with the Big Bad Banksia Men of May Gibbs's Snugglepot and Cuddlepie, whose gumnut hats are also put to good use in the artist's studio. Each piece is selected with a rapacious greedy eye—this can be good for something ... maybe ... sometime. Each provides some natural informality that, when applied to clay, gives something to push against—physically and conceptually—to fill and shape.

Fuller's studio has begun to fill with this detritus of her daily walks, of small, beautiful seeds, bark and objects she has begun to collect and covet. It's a nice way to think of her there, surrounded by all these things, thoughts, half-remembered shapes and sensations. All those pots, always something to do, the grow and flow. Where the ephemeral becomes a thing to savour, and, once fired and fixed, to last forever.

—— **Glenn Barkley**

39 It would be worth mentioning here some other Australian artists—primarily painters—who have maintained a studio-based painting practice whilst establishing an extensive body of work in the ceramic medium. This would include artists such as Karen Black, Belinda Fox (in collaboration with Neville French) and Angela Brennan.

40 This lack of training continues to create some anxiety within the Australian and international ceramics world, not specifically in regard to Fuller but to the wave of contemporary ceramicists who chose to see not technique and arcane methodology as the key principle of making but who rather foreground immediacy and contemporary political and social concerns.

41 A distinction made clear in the masterly installation designed by Khai Liew for Fuller's exhibition at the Samstag Museum, 4 March—27 May 2022. Liew picked up on these streams, choosing a detail which was then repeated over and over, and, when installed in the low light space of the gallery, resembled a dense celestial canopy.

42 Conversation with the artist, 15/12/22.

43 Op. cit.

44 Bennetts was established in 1887 by Charles William Bennett and is currently in its fifth generation of family ownership. They describe their terracotta thus: "a beautiful warm terracotta colour that only nature can produce having come from the earth here in South Australia". https://bennettsmagillpottery.com.au/pottery-categories/product/18-terracotta-clay.html, accessed 6/1/23.

45 ibid. A great description for a sensation anyone who has worked with Bennetts terracotta would understand.

46 Fuller was part of a group led by archaeologist Don Hein and AGSA curator Dick Richards. Some of the material excavated during this period from the 1970s to the 1980s is now in AGSA's collection, and was first exhibited in *Thai Ceramics: Bang Chiang, Khmer, Sawankhalok Ceramics* (1977), Art Gallery of South Australia.

47 'Walking', Thomas Traherne, date unknown https://www.poetryfoundation.org/poems/45417/walking-56d22507720e9, accessed 6/1/23.

48 If you want to also get a sense of these walks, you can also follow Fuller's Instagram account which now acts as an ongoing visual diary or sketchbook of suburban Adelaide and the artist's meandering.

Helen Fuller: Pots

2009

Helen Fuller

2023

Timeline 2009 —— 2023

2009 ¶ Artist and writer Stephanie Radok introduces Fuller to Pat Brooks' beginner pottery class at the celebrated Ruth Tuck Art School. Fuller creates new forms of art, including simulated boxed paper pots, made by cutting up and weaving leftover invitations from her solo exhibition *beauty and the beast* at Place Gallery. Artworks in several Sullivan+Strumpf exhibitions. Annabelle Collett includes her in Prospect Gallery's (now Newmarch Gallery) *Third Design Biennial* of contemporary textile works.

2010 ——— 2011 ¶ Fuller holds her first solo ceramics show of 76 hand-built terracotta pots at Pembroke School, following an artist-in-residency, and also exhibits pots in the exhibition *Consumed*, curated by Ingrid Kellenbach, at Adelaide Central Gallery. Wins the South Australian Potters' Guild Ceramics Award, judged by Gerry Wedd, with a work subsequently acquired by AGSA. Reviewing the Award in *The Journal of Australian Ceramics*, Stephen Bowers described Fuller as an 'ingénue', due to her newness to the field. ¶ Spends time at Koonalda Cave on the Nullarbor Plains as a volunteer fieldwork photographer with the archaeologist Dr Keryn Walshe, later showing pots inspired by the excursion in a solo exhibition, *Winding Threads,* at Adelaide Central Gallery. Begins a three-year tenancy at JamFactory's Ceramic Studio.

Helen Fuller

2012 ——— 2013 ¶ Demonstrates ceramic techniques at the exhibition *2012 Australian Ceramics Triennale: Subversive Clay,* held in Adelaide. Meets Stephen Benwell, whose pots had inspired her in 1983, and exhibits in *Subvert* at Light Square Gallery, Adelaide. Holds exhibitions at Place Gallery as well as at BMG in Adelaide, JamFactory, Adelaide Central Gallery and Adelaide Festival Centre's Artspace. Flinders Foundation acquire fourteen of Fuller's paintings for their Centre for Innovation in Cancer. Mentors Aleksandra Antic and travels with Dr Keryn Walshe to Seal Bay on Kangaroo Island. Travels to the Philippines with ceramicist Mark Valenzuela—a JamFactory Ceramic Studio colleague—and exhibits at Artinformal Gallery in Manila.

2014 ¶ At the invitation of Terence Maloon, presents fifty pots in a solo exhibition at the Drill Hall Gallery, Australian National University, Canberra. Exhibits with Kirsten Coelho and Bruce Nuske at Aptos Cruz Galleries, Adelaide. Selected as a finalist in the 29th Gold Coast International Ceramic Art Award, which acquires her work. Exhibits in *Important Exhibition of Australian Ceramics,* Mossgreen Gallery, Victoria, a tribute exhibition to Janet Mansfield OAM, curated by Prue Venables. Travels again to South East Asia, participating in *Tropical Blaze*, a biannual international ceramics conference, held at the studio of Pablo Capati III in San Jose, Batangas, Philippines, in partnership with the University of the Philippines. Shows in *Bond Klay Keramic II: The 2nd International Contemporary Ceramic Art Exhibition,* Lak Muang Gallery, Thailand.

Timeline 2009 —— 2023

2015 ——— 2016 ¶ Participates in the *City of Hobart Art Prize* and in *Return to Beauty,* curated by Vipoo Srivilasa at Edwina Corlette Gallery, Brisbane. Presents work with Kirsten Coelho and Patsy Hely in *Collect* at JamFactory. Peta Mount discusses Fuller's ceramic work, fired in a Japanese anagama wood-fuelled kiln, in Guildhouse's *Well Made*. With Mark Valenzuela, Benjie Ranada and Alvin Tan Teck Heng, guides two-week mentorships in the Philippines for international and local ceramicists, culminating in *Tropical Blaze: Amihan*, Start Gallery, University Philippines Centre for Fine Arts. Responds to the significant bushfire damage to red gums around Angaston, South Australia, in *Silent Nature* at JamFactory's Seppeltsfield Gallery. Fuller and Zhu divorce.

2017 ——— 2019 ¶ Visits Japan with ceramist friend Michael Ferrier. Joins a small women-only group textile tour in Vietnam. As an artist-in-residence, exhibits at Foundation University in the Philippines. At curators Glenn Barkley and Holly Williams's invitation, presents work in the *National Self-Portrait Prize* at UQ Art Museum in 2017. Exhibits with mentee and ceramicist Nerida Bell in *Warps and Wefts* at Adelaide Central Gallery, and they jointly publish on their process in *The Journal of Australian Ceramics*. Reunites with textile artist Kay Lawrence and printmaker Olga Sankey—four decades after exhibiting together at the *Adelaide Festival of Arts*—in the joint exhibition *Drawing on Material Things* at West Gallery Thebarton, Adelaide, which explores the spontaneous gesture of the line. Returns to Pembroke School as the artist-in-residence.

2020 ——— 2021 ¶ COVID-19 lockdowns are introduced in Sydney one day after Fuller's *Coil Pots* exhibition opens at Darlinghurst's Stanley Street Gallery, effectively ending the show. She devotes significant time to Antony Hamilton, now terminally ill. Hamilton passes away on 9 October 2020, and bequeaths Fuller his house at Beltana, Flinders Ranges, which she plans potentially to turn into an artists' residence, assisted by her younger brother Stan. Grants permission for the Day Street Surf Club mural, painted when she was aged sixteen, to be reinterpreted in Ocean Parade, Middleton, by Barbary O'Brien.

2022 ¶ Samstag Museum of Art presents *Helen Fuller*, a large and ethereal display of the artist's recent ceramics, for the 2022 Adelaide Festival. Designer Khai Liew creates an unusual, immersive environment for the artwork display. The exhibition is widely acknowledged a critical and artistic triumph. Both AGSA and the Powerhouse Museum in Sydney acquire several works as a result. ¶ Begins mentoring the Ngarrindjeri, Ngadjuri, Narungga and Wirangu weaver and artist Sonya Rankine. At friend Bill Robinson's request, writes a catalogue memoir for his exhibition *Love in Life & Art* at the William Robinson Gallery, QUT Museum, Brisbane, celebrating the life of his late wife Shirley. ¶ Awarded the 2023 South Australian Living Artist (SALA) Monograph publication.

Timeline 2009 —— 2023

Helen Fuller, *Untitled*, 2014, hand-built terracotta with underglaze, oxide, porcelain slip. Collection Mary Eagle. Photograph Michael Field, image courtesy Drill Hall Gallery, Canberra.

Helen Fuller

097

Works

Helen Fuller

Helen Fuller, 2014, hand-built terracotta with underglaze, oxide, porcelain slip. Collection the artist.
Photograph Michael Field, images courtesy Drill Hall Gallery, Canberra.

Works

Helen Fuller, *Untitled*, 2014, hand-built terracotta, oxide, porcelain slip. Private Collection. Photograph Michael Field, images courtesy Drill Hall Gallery, Canberra.

Helen Fuller, *Untitled*, 2014, hand-built terracotta, oxide, porcelain slip. Private Collection.
Photograph Michael Field, image courtesy Drill Hall Gallery, Canberra.

Helen Fuller

Helen Fuller, 2020, terracotta with underglaze, oxides, porcelain slip, wire, sandalwood. Collection the artist. Photograph Grant Hancock.

Helen Fuller

Helen Fuller, 2020, terracotta with underglaze, oxides, porcelain slip, wire, sandalwood. Collection the artist. Photograph Grant Hancock.

Helen Fuller, 2021, hand-built terracotta, oxide, porcelain slip. Collection the artist.
Photograph Grant Hancock.

Helen Fuller, 2021, hand-built terracotta, oxide, porcelain slip. Collection Ross Wolfe.
Photograph Grant Hancock.

Works

Helen Fuller, 2021, hand-built terracotta, oxide, porcelain slip. Collection Ross Wolfe.
Photograph Grant Hancock.

Helen Fuller

Works

Helen Fuller, 2021, hand-built terracotta, oxide, porcelain slip.
Collection the artist. Photograph Grant Hancock.

Helen Fuller

Helen Fuller, 2021, hand-built terracotta, oxides. Collection the artist.
Photograph Grant Hancock.

Helen Fuller, 2021, hand-built terracotta, porcelain slip. Collection Ross Wolfe.
Photograph Grant Hancock.

Helen Fuller, 2021, hand-built terracotta, oxide, porcelain slip.
Collection the artist. Photograph Grant Hancock.

Works

Helen Fuller, 2022, installation view, 2022 Adelaide Festival exhibition with Khai Liew, Samstag Museum of Art. Photograph Grant Hancock.

Works

Helen Fuller, 2022, hand-built terracotta, oxides, porcelain slip.
Private Collection. Photograph Grant Hancock.

Helen Fuller, *Two Vessels*, 2022, detail, hand-built terracotta, oxides, porcelain slip. Powerhouse Collection. Purchased with funds from the Barry Willoughby Bequest and Powerhouse Foundation, 2022. Photograph Grant Hancock.

Works

Helen Fuller, 2021, hand-built terracotta, oxide, porcelain slip. Collection the artist.
Photograph Grant Hancock.

Helen Fuller

Works

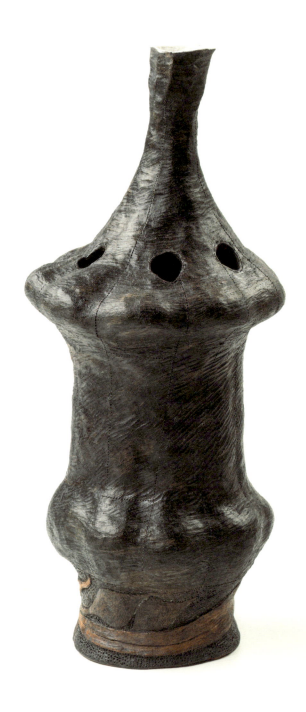

Helen Fuller, 2021, hand-built terracotta, oxides, porcelain slip. Collection the artist.
Photograph Grant Hancock.

Helen Fuller

Helen Fuller, 2021, hand-built terracotta, oxides, porcelain slip.
Collection the artist. Photograph Grant Hancock.

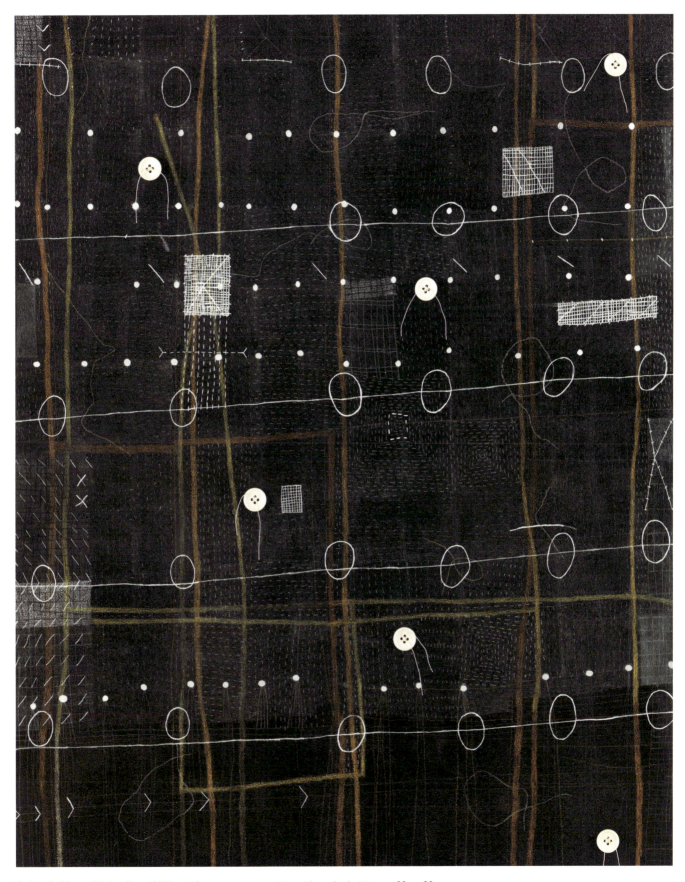

Helen Fuller, *Night Sky*, 2021, oil on canvas, cotton thread, buttons, 60 x 90 cm. Collection Khai Liew. Photograph Grant Hancock.

Works

Helen Fuller, 2021, hand-built terracotta with underglaze, oxides, porcelain slip. Private Collection. Photograph Grant Hancock.

Helen Fuller, *Hand-built vessel*, 2021, terracotta with underglaze, oxides, porcelain slip, 21.6 x 21.7 x 22.7 cm. Art Gallery of South Australia Collection. Edward Minton Newman Bequest Fund 2022. Photograph Grant Hancock. 2023 SALA Poster image.

Works

Samstag Museum of Art
Acknowledgements

This publication has its origin in an exhibition, *Helen Fuller*, presented in collaboration with Khai Liew by the Samstag Museum of Art during the 2022 Adelaide Festival. The critical and popular success of the exhibition inspired a successful proposal, made by Samstag to Arts SA, that Helen Fuller be awarded the 2023 SALA Monograph, in association with Wakefield Press. Accordingly, the Samstag Museum of Art expresses grateful appreciation to Arts SA, the Government of South Australia, the Board and staff of the South Australian Living Artists Festival, and Wakefield Press for their ongoing commitment to this valuable series of publications, which has made such beneficial contributions to the careers and reputations of leading South Australian artists.

We especially thank Rhana Devenport ONZM, Director, Art Gallery of South Australia, and Dr Lisa Slade, Assistant Director, Artistic Programs, for their generous agreement to officially host Helen Fuller as the featured artist for the 2023 SALA Festival, and the monograph's public launch in Adelaide. We similarly thank Vanessa Van Ooyen, Director, QUT Galleries and Museums at Queensland University of Technology, for undertaking to launch the monograph in Brisbane, in conjunction with QUT's exhibition of Helen Fuller's work.

The Samstag Museum gratefully acknowledges the many public galleries, institutions and private collectors that have kindly granted image permissions for Helen Fuller's works of art from their collections or from past exhibitions—in many instances also arranging the photography—including: Artbank; Art Gallery of South Australia; Drill Hall Gallery, Australian National University; Griffith University Art Museum; National Gallery of Australia; National Gallery of Victoria; Museum of Applied Arts & Sciences, Powerhouse Museum; Queensland Art Gallery, Gallery of Modern Art; QUT Art Museum; The University of Queensland Art Museum; Lawrence Wilson Art Gallery, The University of Western Australia; and Helen Watters, Ingrid Kellenbach, Mary Eagle, Ross Wolfe and Khai Liew.

Among others whose assistance has played an essential part in bringing the publication to fruition, the Samstag Museum extends warm thanks to Grant Hancock for his skill and reliability in photographing Helen Fuller's work. We are indebted as well to text editor Lia Weston for her meticulous reading of the writers' texts and her always-pertinent suggestions, and to editorial consultant Eve Sullivan for her cogent advice during the development of the publication. We express appreciation to Melinda Rackham for her patient research in compiling images and for her consultative acumen in developing the informative chronology of the artist's key lifetime events and exhibitions.

In seeking a fresh approach to the publication's design, the Samstag Museum turned to our long-time designer Adam Johnson, giving him latitude to craft something innovative. His good judgement has delivered a 2023 SALA Monograph of impressive excellence, for which we are most grateful.

The 2023 SALA Monograph is anchored by expert contributions from three essayists—Ross Wolfe, Sasha Grbich and Glenn Barkley—who have together illuminated the life and art of Helen Fuller in distinctive fashion, and each from very different perspectives. We sincerely appreciate their thoughtful insights, which have ensured a more complete understanding and historical record of the artist than previously existed.

But most importantly, the writers have also revealed the truth of Helen Fuller's deep creative impulse and her enduring propensity for hard work, which is now visible to all, and appropriately celebrated. We applaud and thank her; it's been a delight to work with her.

The Samstag Museum of Art is proud to be associated with such an important initiative, which exemplifies our public cultural role in providing South Australian audiences the educational experience of advanced visual art and, along with this, opportunities for artists to present work in one of Australia's most beautiful and renowned contemporary art museums. We are mindful, in this respect, that the 2023 SALA Monograph would not have been possible without the University of South Australia's continuing financial support of the Samstag Museum and its precursors, a commitment sustained for thirty years in a visionary manner since the University's establishment in 1992.

—— **Erica Green**
Director, Anne & Gordon Samstag Museum of Art,
University of South Australia

Helen Fuller, 2022, installation view,
2022 Adelaide Festival exhibition with Khai Liew,
Samstag Museum of Art.
Photograph Grant Hancock.

Samstag Museum of Art Acknowledgements

Helen Fuller Thanks

I have an abundance of reasons to be grateful for this publication about my life and work as an artist. For it to have happened at all, I am indebted to the Samstag Museum of Art; Arts SA, Government of South Australia; SALA Festival; and Wakefield Press.

A great many people have supported me in the pursuit of my visual arts practice, over many years, in different ways. I especially thank Erica Green, Director of the Samstag Museum of Art, for her incredible belief in my art, and for creating opportunities that have been pivotal to my development at key moments.

I am honoured that the Art Gallery of South Australia will publicly launch the monograph during the 2023 SALA Festival, and that the QUT Galleries and Museums at the Queensland University of Technology in Brisbane—where I once worked—will similarly do so, in conjunction with an exhibition of my work.

For their crucial roles in assisting this publication, I am particularly grateful to the writers, Ross Wolfe, Sasha Grbich and Glenn Barkley, whose wonderful essays have flattered me with their thoughtful insights. I thank Melinda Rackham, too, for her patience and thoroughness in bringing order to my extensive archival history. I am indebted to Grant Hancock, not only for his amazing photographs but also for his aesthetic judgement and excellence. I sincerely thank Adam Johnson, the graphic designer, who has brought everything together in such a masterful and memorable way.

There have been many teachers, friends and colleagues who have inspired and guided my life journey. Some have also given me sustaining support in the face of life's adversities and challenges.

Several loyal friendships, particularly, have been of importance to me, and I warmly thank Julie Blyfield and Kirsten Coelho for their unfailing encouragement, and that of my pyro-clay buddy, Mark Valenzuela, who introduced me to his fellow artists in Batangas, Philippines, and Michael Ferrier from Pembroke School. I will not forget Stephen Rainbird's critical impact on my career, nor the sage, collaborative enthusiasm of Khai Liew, a source for me of great self-belief and confidence, and I thank them both.

In my early years as an art student at the South Australian School of Art, I benefited from the quiet, kindly direction of Helen McIntosh, and the lively creative dialogue with Tony Bishop, a truly generous mentor. It was Tony who introduced me to my friend, the artist Antony Hamilton, and to my original gallerist, the remarkable Ray Hughes, at whose gallery in Brisbane I met William Robinson and Merve Muhling. It was these artists, teachers and colleagues—all lasting friends—whose support secured the beginning of my professional career in 1979.

Finally, I acknowledge my siblings—Trevor, Stan and Kip Fuller—and my son Alexander Fuller-Zhu, for their love and unflagging support in sharing my life, and my journey in art.

It is all a marvellous and beautiful thing, and humbling.

—— ***Helen Fuller,*** February 2023

Helen in her Goodwood studio, 2017.
Photograph David Campbell.

Artist Helen Fuller Thanks

Writer Biographies

Ross Wolfe

Ross Wolfe is an Adelaide-based administrator and writer. He has held influential roles in Australian arts administration, including as director of the Visual Arts Board, Australia Council, from 1983, where he secured formal Italian and Australian government agreements for a permanent Australian Pavilion at the Venice Biennale. An activist in his early career, he founded the seminal visual arts journal, *Art Network* magazine, in 1979, and was closely involved with establishment of Artspace, in Sydney. Wolfe was deputy director at the Art Gallery of South Australia from 1988 and, from 1992—2009, inaugural director of the philanthropic Samstag Program at the University of South Australia. He is a regular contributor of articles and reviews to Australian visual arts journals, and is the author and editor of *The Samstag Legacy: An Artist's Bequest*, a 2016 biography of Anne and Gordon Samstag.

Sasha Grbich

Sasha Grbich is an artist, writer and lecturer at the Adelaide Central School of Art where she teaches in sculpture, art history and theory. Grbich is a regular contributor to *Artlink* and other critical review publications. She was awarded the 2018 Anne & Gordon Samstag International Visual Arts Scholarship to attend the Maumaus School's School of Visual Art in Portugal, and undertook this institution's independent study program. In 2015, Grbich completed postgraduate research at University of South Australia. She is currently researching her PhD at Flinders University, addressing women's experimental art practices in 1970s Australia through the Flinders University Museum of Art's collection of post-object and documentation art collection.

Helen Fuller

—— **_Glenn Barkley_**

Glenn Barkley is a Sydney-based independent curator, artist and valuer. He was previously senior curator at the Museum of Contemporary Art Australia from 2008 to 2014, and curator of the University of Wollongong Art Collection from 1996 to 2007. Between 2007 and 2008, he was director and curator of the Ergas Collection. Barkley is currently an Associate Curator of The Curators' Department, Sydney, which is the organisation he co-founded in 2015. He has written extensively on Australian art and culture for magazines such as _Art Monthly Australasia_, _Artist Profile_ and _Art + Australia_, as well as for numerous catalogues and monographs. Barkley has a diverse area of interest and knowledge, including: ceramics; public art; artist books and ephemera; outsider art and other marginal art forms; public and private collection management and development; and horticulture. He is currently writing a global history of ceramics to be published by Thames & Hudson in late 2023.

Writer Biographies

Helen Fuller